~A BINGO BOOK~

Nevada
Bingo Book

COMPLETE BINGO GAME IN A BOOK

Written By Rebecca Stark

ISBN 978-0-87386-521-0

Educational Books 'n' Bingo

Printed in the U.S.A.

DIRECTIONS

INCLUDED:

List of Terms

Templates for Additional Terms and Clues

2 Clues per Term

30 Unique Bingo Sheets (To cut out or copy)

Sheet of Markers (to copy and distribute)

1. **Either cut apart the book or make copies of ALL the sheets. You might want to make an extra copy of the clue sheets to use for introduction and review. Keep the sheets in an envelope for easy reuse.**

2. Cut apart the call sheets with terms and clues.

3. Pass out one bingo sheet per student. There are enough unique sheets for a class of 30.

4. Pass out the markers. You may cut apart the markers included in this book or use any other small items of your choice. Students can also mark the sheets themselves; recopy the sheets as needed for additional games.

5. Decide whether or not you will require the entire sheet to be filled. Requiring the entire sheet to be filled provides a better review. However, if you have a short time to fill, you may prefer to have them do the just the border or some other format. Tell the class before you begin what is required.

6. There are 50 terms. Read the list before you begin. If there are any terms that have not been covered in class, you may want to read to the students the term and clues before you begin.

7. There is a blank space in the middle of each sheet. You can instruct the students to use it as a free space or you can write in answers to cover terms not included. Of course, in this case you would create your own clues. (Templates provided.)

8. Shuffle the sheets and place them in a pile. Two or three clues are provided for each term. If you plan to play the game with the same group more than once, you might want to choose a different clue for each game. If not, you may choose to use more than one clue.

9. Be sure to keep the sheets you have used for the present game in a separate pile. When a student calls, "Bingo," he or she will have to verify that the correct answers are on his or her sheet AND that the markers were placed in response to the proper questions. Pull out the sheets that are on the student's sheet keeping them in the order they were used in the game. Read each clue as it was given and ask the student to identify the correct answer from his or her sheet.

10. If the student has the correct answers on the sheet AND has shown that they were marked in response to the *correct questions,* then that student is the winner and the game is over. If the student does not have the correct answers on the sheet OR he or she marked the answers in response to *the wrong questions,* then the game continues until there is a proper winner.

11. If you want to play again, reshuffle the sheets and begin again.

Have fun

TERMS

Basin and Range

Battle Born State

Border(s)

Boundary Peak

Kit Carson

Carson City

Columbia Plateau

Comstock Lode

County (-ies)

Dayton

Desert Bighorn

Desert Tortoise

Executive Branch

Flag

John C. Frémont

Gemstone

Great Basin National Park

Henderson

Hoover Dam

Ichthyosaur

Indian Rice Grass

Industry (-ies)

Judicial Branch

Lake Mead

Lake Tahoe

Las Vegas

Legislative Branch

Livestock

Mining (-ed)

Motto

Mountain Bluebird

Mustang(s)

Pueblo Grande de Nevada

Quarter

Reno

Reservation

River(s)

Sagebrush

Sandstone

Seal

Sierra Nevada

Silver

Song

State

Trees

Tule Duck Decoy

Mark Twain

Virginia & Truckee Railroad

Virginia City

Sarah Winnemucca

Additional Terms

Choose as many additional terms as you would like and write them in the
squares. Repeat each as desired.
Cut out the squares and randomly distribute them to the class.
Instruct the students to place their square on the center space of their card.

© Barbara M. Peller

Clues for Additional Terms

Write three clues for each of your additional terms.

_____ 1. _____ 2. _____ 3. _____	_____ 1. _____ 2. _____ 3. _____
_____ 1. _____ 2. _____ 3. _____	_____ 1. _____ 2. _____ 3. _____
_____ 1. _____ 2. _____ 3. _____	_____ 1. _____ 2. _____ 3. _____

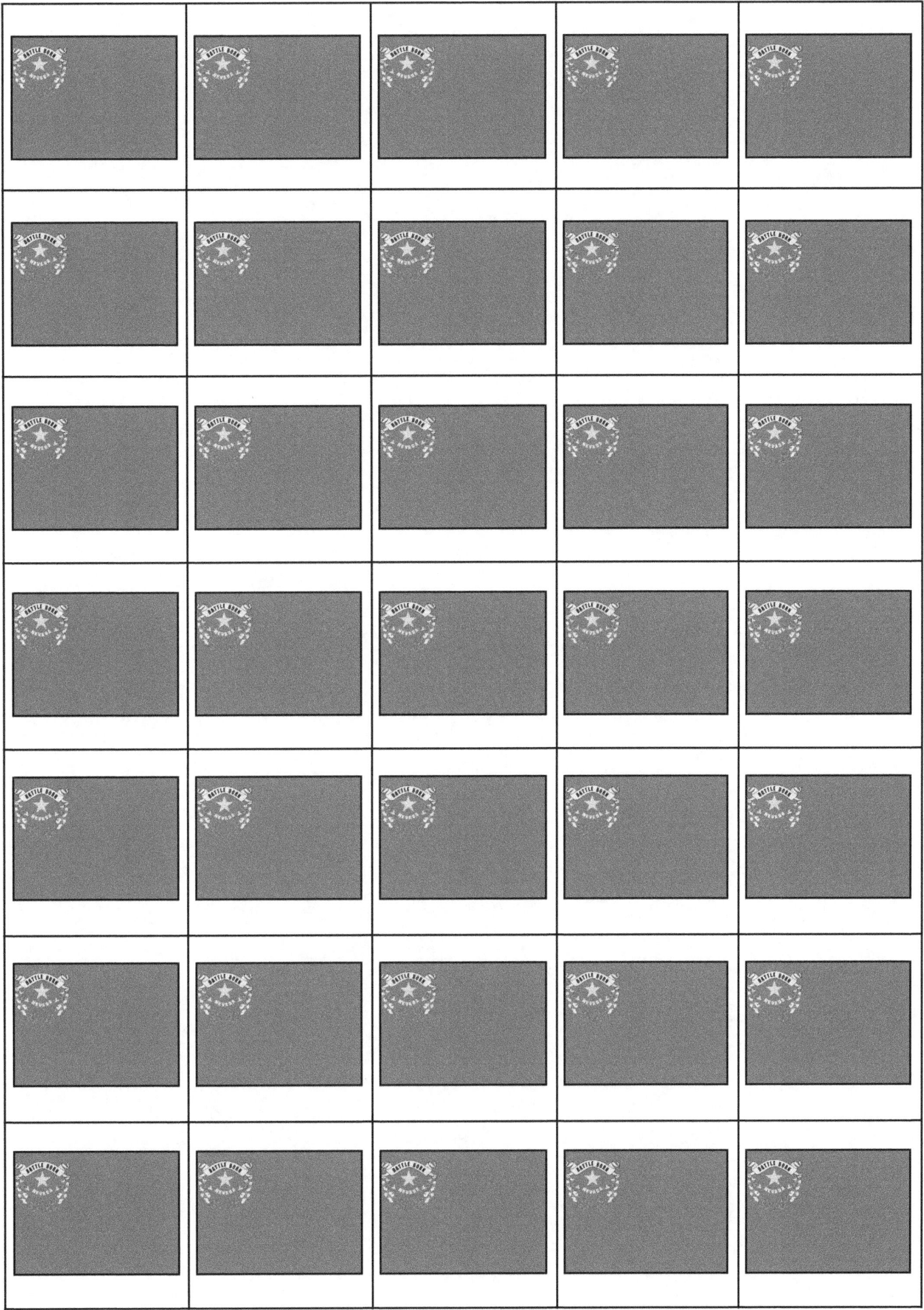

Basin and Range
1. Most of Nevada is in the ___ Region. A series of mountain ranges run parallel to low, broad valleys.
2. The Toiyabe, Toquima, Snake, and Toana mountain ranges are in this geographic region. Scattered among the ranges are buttes and mesas as well as flat valleys.

Battle Born State
1. This slogan is on the state flag.
2. This phrase, which is on the state flag, refers to the fact that Nevada was admitted to the Union during the Civil War.

Border(s)
1. Arizona, California, Idaho, Oregon, and Utah ___ Nevada.
2. Lake Tahoe is on the California-Nevada ___.

Boundary Peak
1. At 13,140 feet, ___ is the highest point in the state.
2. ___ is in the White Mountains near the California border. Some consider it a sub-peak of Montgomery Peak, which is in California.

Kit Carson
1. This frontiersman was a hunter, trapper, and guide. The capital of the state is named after him.
2. ___ was hired by John C. Frémont of the Army Corps of Engineers as a guide. He led Frémont through California, Oregon, and the Great Basin National Park area.

Carson City
1. ___ is the capital of Nevada. It was named after Christopher Houston Carson, better known as Kit Carson.
2. ___ originated as a stopover for emigrants on their way to California. It grew into a city when silver ore was discovered nearby under what is now Virginia City.

Columbia Plateau
1. Nevada can be divided into three main geographic regions: the Sierra Nevada, the Basin and Range, and the ___.
2. The ___ is in the northeastern corner of Nevada. There are deep canyons with steep ridges. Near the Idaho border the land turns to open prairie.

Comstock Lode
1. The ___ was the first major discovery of silver ore in the United States.
2. The ___ was located under what is now Virginia City.

County (-ies)
1. There are 16 ___ and one independent city. The independent city is Carson City.
2. More than two-thirds of Nevada's residents live in Clark ___.

Dayton
1. ___ is the site of the first gold discovery in 1849.
2. ___ and Genoa each claims to be the first settlement in Nevada. Both are near Carson City and both were settled in 1851.

Nevada Bingo

© Barbara M. Peller

Desert Bighorn
1. The ___, or Nelson, sheep is the state animal.
2. This mammal is well-suited for Nevada's mountainous desert country because it can survive for long periods without water.

Desert Tortoise
1. The ___ is the state reptile. It is the largest reptile in the southwestern United States.
2. This reptile lives in the extreme southern parts of Nevada. It lives in underground burrows to escape the harsh summer heat and winter cold.

Executive Branch
1. The governor, lieutenant governor, secretary of state, state treasurer, state controller, and attorney general are all part of the ___.
2. The governor is the head of the ___. The present-day governor is [fill in].

Flag
1. The state ___ has a cobalt blue field. In the upper left is a five-pointed silver star. Sagebrush, the state flower, is below the star.
2. Across the top of the sagebrush on the state ___ is a scroll with the words "Battle Born." The name "Nevada" is beneath the star.

John C. Frémont
1. Explorer ___ traveled through Western Nevada, including the future site of Carson City. He named the river flowing through the valley after his scout, Kit Carson.
2. He is known as the Pathfinder.

Gemstone
1. The official state precious ___ is the black fire opal. The Virgin Valley in northern Nevada is the only place in North America where significant amounts are found.
2. The official state semi-precious ___ is Nevada turquoise, sometimes called the "jewel of the desert."

Great Basin National Park
1. Wheeler Park and Lehman Caves are main attractions of the ___.
2. Lehman Caves cavern is in the ___. This beautiful marble cave is decorated with stalactites, stalagmites, helictites, and other formations.

Henderson
1. ___ is the second largest city in Nevada. It is in the Las Vegas metropolitan area.
2. The Las Vegas metropolitan area includes 3 of the 4 most populous cities in the state: Las Vegas, ___, and North Las Vegas. Reno, which is in a different part of the state, is the third most populous.

Hoover Dam
1. ___ is a concrete, arch-gravity dam in the Black Canyon of the Colorado River. It is on the border between Arizona and Nevada.
2. Once known as Boulder Dam, ___ was the world's largest dam at the time of its construction in the 1930s.

Ichthyosaur
1. The ___ is the state fossil
2. Nevada is the only state to possess a complete skeleton of this extinct marine reptile.

Nevada Bingo

Indian Rice Grass
1. ___ is the state grass.
2. ___ was once a staple food source for Native Americans of the region. They ground the grain into flour to make bread.

Industry (-ies)
1. Tourism and mining are important ___ in the state.
2. Nevada's service ___—especially gambling, amusement and recreational services—are very important. These services are concentrated in the Las Vegas and Reno metropolitan areas.

Judicial Branch
1. The ___ interprets what our laws mean and makes decisions about the laws and those who break them.
2. The Supreme Court is the highest court in the ___ of the state government.

Lake Mead
1. Damming the Colorado River created ___.
2. Formed by the Hoover Dam along the Colorado River, the National Park Service established ___ as a national recreation area in 1964.

Lake Tahoe
1. This beautiful glacial lake in the Sierra Nevada is located along the border between California and Nevada.
2. ___ is the largest alpine lake in North America. This beautiful, clear lake is surrounded by mountains on all sides.

Las Vegas
1. ___ is the largest city in the state and the largest city in the Mojave Desert.
2. ___ calls itself the "Entertainment Capital of the World." The ___ Strip is outside the city limits. It passes through the unincorporated towns of Paradise and Winchester.

Legislative Branch
1. The ___ of government comprises the Senate and the Assembly.
2. The ___ makes the laws.

Livestock
1. Ranching is the most important agricultural activity, and cattle and sheep are the most important ___ products. Other ___ products are hogs and lamb.
2. Alfalfa is the most harvested crop in Nevada. Alfalfa hay is used mostly to feed ___.

Mining (-ed)
1. Nevada leads the nation in the ___ of gold and silver.
2. The most valuable ___ product in the state is gold.

Motto
1. The state ___ is "All For Our Country."
2. The inner circle of the state's Great Seal has the ___ "All for Our Country."

Mountain Bluebird 1. The ____ is the state bird. 2. This songbird is a member of the thrush family. Males are identified by a bright blue color on the upper part of their bodies. Females have blue wings and a slight grayish color.	**Mustang(s)** 1. Three ____ are depicted on the state quarter. More than half of all ____ in North America are found in Nevada. 2. The ____ is a free-roaming horse; it was first brought to the Americas by the Spanish.
Pueblo Grande de Nevada 1. ____ was occupied by the Anasazi and other groups between 300 and 1150. It is sometimes called "Nevada's Lost City." It is listed on the National Register of Historic Places. 2. Several of the houses in the ____ had up to 20 rooms, with the largest having 100 rooms!	**Quarter** 1. Nevada's state ____ depicts three mustangs, the sun rising behind snow-capped mountains, and sagebrush. 2. A banner that reads "The Silver State" is on the state ____.
Reno 1. ____ is the third largest city in Nevada. It calls itself the "Biggest Little City in the World." 2. This city in Washoe County is in a high desert valley at the foot of the Sierra Nevada.	**Reservation** 1. The Pyramid Lake Indian ____ and the Walker Lake Indian ____ are governed by Northern Paiute tribes. 2. Duck Valley Indian ____ is on the Idaho-Nevada state line. It was established as a homeland for the Shoshone and Paiute tribes.
River(s) 1. The Colorado, Columbia, Humboldt, and Truckee are important ____ in the state. 2. The Humboldt ____ is the longest in the state and the second longest in the Great Basin. It runs from northeastern Nevada through Winnemucca.	**Sagebrush** 1. ____ is the state flower. It has gray-green twigs and pale yellow flowers. 2. ____ grows where other kinds of vegetation cannot. It is an important winter food for sheep and cattle.
Sandstone 1. ____ is the state rock. 2. This sedimentary rock is what provides the spectacular scenery of Valley of Fire State Park and Red Rock Canyon Recreational Lands.	**Seal** 1. The picture in the Great ____ includes representations of mining, agriculture, industry, and scenery of Nevada. 2. Beneath the picture on the Great ____ is the state motto, "All For Our Country."

Nevada Bingo

© Barbara M. Peller

Sierra Nevada
1. This rugged mountain range cuts across part of Nevada south of Carson City.
2. Lake Tahoe, a beautiful glacial lake on the California-Nevada border, lies in one of the valleys of the Sierra Nevada.

Silver
1. ___ is the state metal. One of the state's nicknames is the "___ State."
2. The Comstock Lode was the first major discovery of ___ ore in the United States.

Song
1. The state ___ is "Home Means Nevada."
2. In addition to a state ___, there is also a state march. It is "Silver State Fanfare."

State
1. Before Nevada became a ___, it was part of Utah Territory and Nevada Territory.
2. When Nevada was admitted to the Union on October 31, 1864, it became the 36th state.

Trees
1. There are two state ___: the single-leaf piñon and the bristlecone pine.
2. Both of the state ___ are pines. Bristlecone pines are thought to live longer than any other living thing on Earth.

Tule Duck Decoy
1. The ___ is the state artifact. There are eleven.
2. Created by early Nevadans almost 2,000 years ago, each ___ is formed of a bundle of bullrush stems, bound together and shaped to resemble a canvasback duck.

Mark Twain
1. This author's real name was Samuel Clemens.
2. ___ lived in Virginia City and Carson City from 1861 to 1864. He was working at the *Territorial Enterprise,* a newspaper published in Virginia City, when he adopted this pen name.

Virginia & Truckee Railroad
1. The ___ connected Reno with Carson City, Virginia City, and Minden.
2. The ___ hauled valuable Comstock ore to quartz-reduction mills located at Silver City and along the Carson River.

Virginia City
1. ___ became a boomtown as a result of the Comstock Lode.
2. ___ maintains several buildings and artifacts that remain from the time it was a boomtown. Because of this, ___ draws over 2 million visitors per year.

Sarah Winnemucca
1. ___'s autobiographical work, *Life Among the Piutes: Their Wrongs and Claims,* was originally published in 1883.
2. ___ dedicated her life to improving the living conditions of her people. Her writings described Northern Paiute life and the impact of white settlement.

Nevada Bingo

Nevada Bingo

Sagebrush	Basin and Range	Border(s)	Ichthyosaur	Kit Carson
Henderson	Battle Born State	Virginia & Truckee Railroad	Motto	Sierra Nevada
Mark Twain	Mining (-ed)		Reno	Virginia City
Tule Duck Decoy	Seal	Trees	Livestock	Mustang(s)
Quarter	Judicial Branch	John C. Frémont	Song	Lake Tahoe

Nevada Bingo: Card No. 1

Nevada Bingo

Tule Duck Decoy	Mark Twain	County (-ies)	Sandstone	Legislative Branch
Mustang(s)	Gemstone	Comstock Lode	Seal	Pueblo Grande de Nevada
Desert Bighorn	Judicial Branch		Lake Mead	Trees
Reservation	River(s)	Mining (-ed)	Sarah Winnemucca	Kit Carson
Sierra Nevada	Virginia & Truckee Railroad	John C. Frémont	Henderson	Song

Nevada Bingo: Card No. 2

Nevada Bingo

Judicial Branch	Trees	Gemstone	Livestock	Mark Twain
Mustang(s)	Battle Born State	Dayton	Basin and Range	Industry (-ies)
Seal	Virginia & Truckee Railroad		Pueblo Grande de Nevada	Boundary Peak
Mining (-ed)	Desert Bighorn	Quarter	Reservation	County (-ies)
Song	Desert Tortoise	John C. Frémont	Sarah Winnemucca	Legislative Branch

Nevada Bingo: Card No. 3

Nevada Bingo

Mining (-ed)	Pueblo Grande de Nevada	Border(s)	Desert Tortoise	Legislative Branch
Mountain Bluebird	Columbia Plateau	Basin and Range	Sandstone	Mark Twain
Reno	Reservation		Lake Tahoe	Ichthyosaur
Trees	Battle Born State	Virginia & Truckee Railroad	John C. Frémont	Comstock Lode
Executive Branch	Sierra Nevada	Carson City	Song	Virginia City

Nevada Bingo: Card No. 4

Nevada Bingo

Sierra Nevada	Kit Carson	Seal	Comstock Lode	Desert Tortoise
Mountain Bluebird	Trees	Dayton	Lake Mead	Battle Born State
Border(s)	Virginia City		Motto	Indian Rice Grass
Lake Tahoe	Legislative Branch	Sagebrush	Sarah Winnemucca	Flag
Gemstone	John C. Frémont	Mark Twain	Mining (-ed)	Reno

Nevada Bingo

Boundary Peak	Pueblo Grande de Nevada	County (-ies)	Legislative Branch	Virginia City
Livestock	Seal	Flag	Basin and Range	Mark Twain
Sandstone	Executive Branch		Columbia Plateau	Lake Mead
John C. Frémont	Quarter	Sarah Winnemucca	Carson City	Border(s)
Mustang(s)	Comstock Lode	Sagebrush	Reno	Great Basin National Park

Nevada Bingo: Card No. 6

Nevada Bingo

Sagebrush	Pueblo Grande de Nevada	Indian Rice Grass	Trees	Gemstone
Mustang(s)	Legislative Branch	Judicial Branch	Battle Born State	Mountain Bluebird
Virginia City	Ichthyosaur		Lake Mead	Columbia Plateau
Mining (-ed)	Reservation	Dayton	Tule Duck Decoy	Desert Bighorn
John C. Frémont	Desert Tortoise	Sarah Winnemucca	Carson City	Boundary Peak

Nevada Bingo

Reno	Pueblo Grande de Nevada	Hoover Dam	Livestock	Columbia Plateau
Mountain Bluebird	Border(s)	Sandstone	Virginia City	Comstock Lode
Great Basin National Park	Desert Tortoise		Legislative Branch	Kit Carson
Song	Mining (-ed)	Tule Duck Decoy	Executive Branch	Reservation
Virginia & Truckee Railroad	John C. Frémont	Carson City	Seal	Mustang(s)

Nevada Bingo: Card No. 8

Nevada Bingo

Lake Mead	Gemstone	Judicial Branch	Great Basin National Park	Desert Tortoise
Executive Branch	Legislative Branch	Reno	Seal	Pueblo Grande de Nevada
Industry (-ies)	Sagebrush		Battle Born State	Hoover Dam
Flag	Kit Carson	Quarter	Motto	Indian Rice Grass
Reservation	Sarah Winnemucca	Dayton	Tule Duck Decoy	Lake Tahoe

Nevada Bingo

Tule Duck Decoy	Livestock	Columbia Plateau	Sandstone	Great Basin National Park
Virginia City	Comstock Lode	Basin and Range	Battle Born State	Legislative Branch
Desert Tortoise	Pueblo Grande de Nevada		Ichthyosaur	Desert Bighorn
Quarter	Lake Tahoe	Flag	Sarah Winnemucca	Industry (-ies)
Dayton	Mustang(s)	County (-ies)	Sierra Nevada	Reno

Nevada Bingo

Boundary Peak	Pueblo Grande de Nevada	Seal	Flag	Mustang(s)
Hoover Dam	Industry (-ies)	Motto	Lake Mead	Basin and Range
Mountain Bluebird	Legislative Branch		County (-ies)	Judicial Branch
Dayton	Mark Twain	Sarah Winnemucca	Desert Tortoise	Tule Duck Decoy
Executive Branch	John C. Frémont	Sagebrush	Carson City	Gemstone

Nevada
Bingo

Gemstone	Kit Carson	Industry (-ies)	Livestock	Lake Mead
Judicial Branch	Mustang(s)	Border(s)	Carson City	Battle Born State
Sagebrush	Indian Rice Grass		Virginia City	Sandstone
John C. Frémont	Reservation	Legislative Branch	Tule Duck Decoy	Mountain Bluebird
Pueblo Grande de Nevada	Hoover Dam	Desert Tortoise	Executive Branch	Comstock Lode

Nevada Bingo: Card No. 12

Nevada Bingo

Flag	Kit Carson	Boundary Peak	Industry (-ies)	Virginia City
Border(s)	Hoover Dam	Legislative Branch	Lake Mead	Desert Bighorn
Livestock	Comstock Lode		Judicial Branch	Indian Rice Grass
Reno	Sarah Winnemucca	Columbia Plateau	Desert Tortoise	Tule Duck Decoy
John C. Frémont	Lake Tahoe	Carson City	Sagebrush	Motto

Nevada Bingo: Card No. 13

Nevada Bingo

Henderson	Legislative Branch	Seal	Lake Mead	Executive Branch
Comstock Lode	Sagebrush	Industry (-ies)	Battle Born State	Pueblo Grande de Nevada
Flag	Ichthyosaur		County (-ies)	Dayton
Lake Tahoe	Sarah Winnemucca	Desert Tortoise	Columbia Plateau	Boundary Peak
John C. Frémont	Sandstone	Desert Bighorn	Mustang(s)	Reno

Nevada Bingo

Motto	Lake Mead	Seal	Gemstone	Livestock
Boundary Peak	County (-ies)	Basin and Range	Border(s)	Executive Branch
Virginia City	Sagebrush		Mark Twain	Pueblo Grande de Nevada
John C. Frémont	Industry (-ies)	Hoover Dam	Sarah Winnemucca	Flag
Mustang(s)	Reservation	Carson City	Great Basin National Park	Judicial Branch

Nevada Bingo

Columbia Plateau	Industry (-ies)	Hoover Dam	Great Basin National Park	River(s)
Sandstone	Desert Bighorn	Indian Rice Grass	Mountain Bluebird	Ichthyosaur
Flag	Kit Carson		Virginia City	Judicial Branch
Mining (-ed)	Comstock Lode	John C. Frémont	Motto	Tule Duck Decoy
Executive Branch	State	Carson City	Reservation	Pueblo Grande de Nevada

Nevada Bingo: Card No. 16

supply, maintenance, training, and personnel. Table 7-17 provides indicators that leaders can use to identify their strengths and developmental needs in displaying discipline. This document also presents potential underlying causes in failing to model discipline and resources for further development.

Table 7-17. Applies discipline

Strength Indicators	Need Indicators
Applies disciplined initiative in absence of orders. Maintains standards for both self and subordinates. Displays proper time management. Encourages positive behaviors and disciplines negative behaviors.	Displays favoritism and inequality in enforcement of standards. Fails to complete tasks in a timely manner. Fails to execute the Uniform Code of Military Justice properly. Displays non-professional demeanor.
Underlying Causes	
Inability to assess one's own behaviors accurately. Failure to internalize Army Values and traditions. Failure to practice time management. Self-indulgence rather than placing Army priorities first. Lack of understanding of how favoritism undermines authority. Lack of understanding of how to properly communicate and enforce standards.	
Feedback	Select a role model and watch how they demonstrate discipline. Ask how discipline is important to them, what are the pitfalls of slipping standards, how they maintain their self-discipline. Compare how you manage time to others. Do you get as much done as they do or more? Are you prioritizing and getting the most important tasks done on time?
Study	Consider how different types of discipline affect the individual and the unit. Study time management techniques and implement methods to use time efficiently. Review psychological constructs that get in the way of self-discipline (such as ego, restraint defense mechanisms, or delayed gratification). Think about your behaviors and how others might view your self-discipline if they knew what you know about yourself. How would you change your behavior then?
Practice	Consider how others would view your discipline if they were aware of your thoughts/actions; design a plan to fix shortcomings. Establish and stick to a regular exercise routine.

LEADS WITH CONFIDENCE IN ADVERSE SITUATIONS

7-29. The opportunity to lead with confidence in adverse situations happens frequently, but making the right decisions in difficult times defines an Army leader's career. Mistakenly, individuals often believe that leading with confidence in adverse situations is a responsibility for senior leaders, and do not recognize the need for confident leadership at all levels. How Army leaders approach and persevere through difficult times sets a leadership example for others while demonstrating commitment to the organization (see table 7-18 on page 7-20).

Table 7-18. Leads with confidence in adverse situations

Strength Indicators	Need Indicators
Provides presence at the right time and place.	Loses hope or inertia when adversity is high.
Displays self-control and composure in adverse conditions; remains calm under pressure.	Shows discouragement when faced with setbacks.
Remains decisive after discovering a mistake.	Allows anger or emotion to compromise a situation.
Makes decisions; acts in the absence of guidance.	Hesitates to take decisive action; defaults to following a superior's lead in times when it is inappropriate.
Remains positive, even when the situation changes or becomes confusing.	Avoids situations where it is necessary to take an authoritative stand on an issue or problem.
Encourages subordinates.	

Underlying Causes	
Slow to adapt quickly to changing situations.	
Is not comfortable with personal capabilities and skills as a leader; unwilling to step up and take control.	
Is indecisive; has trouble making final decisions.	
Fears that the consequences of making a bad decision will reflect poorly on himself or herself.	
Avoids prudent risks to ensure no negative performance feedback.	
Does not meet problems head-on; is avoidant of conflict.	

Feedback	After leading a difficult mission, conduct an after action review. Ask for feedback to identify effective and ineffective actions and opportunities to improve. Have team members provide feedback on how you handled the situation.
	Request feedback from peers about how well you respond to setbacks, and how effectively you demonstrate persevere to achieve goals.
	Meet with the team to brainstorm creative solutions to a challenge that the organization currently faces. Try to approach the problem from a new and different direction.
	Request advice from a mentor or trusted advisor on how to deal with a difficult situation. Have them guide you and provide insight into possible next steps.
Study	Complete a mission or problem analysis when faced with a tough decision. Consider multiple possible courses of action, select one, and develop a plan of action to enact it.
	Develop the realization that failure and criticism happen. As a leader, take the prudent risk, realizing that you are not always going to be right.
	Learn about planning and problem solving methods and tools to help ensure success.
	Observe a leader who has consistently achieved under seemingly unfavorable circumstances. What behaviors can you model to ensure similar personal success?
	Access the Virtual Improvement Center to complete: Leadership Decision Making; Being an Adaptable Leader in Times of Change; Managing Difficult Behavior
Practice	When resistance occurs, stick to your argument and the facts that support it, while remaining open to feedback and opinions. Remember not to take criticism personally.
	Take on a series of increasingly demanding tasks or challenges to build a record of success and bolster your confidence in difficult situations.
	Be well prepared! Anticipate potential resistance from your audience and spend time gathering data and rationale to support your position.
	Persevere. Do not easily give up on opinions or judgments for which you have a strong argument. Clearly articulate your position using detailed explanations and examples; remain respectful of the opinions of others.
	Use clear, assertive language to state your position. Be aware of nonverbal indicators that may communicate lack of confidence and avoid using tentative language.

DEMONSTRATES TACTICAL AND TECHNICAL COMPETENCE

7-30. Striving for tactical and technical competence and expertise is important for Army leaders. Army leaders must implement the most up-to-date, cutting-edge technologies and methods to solve problems and ensure mission accomplishment. Demonstrating technical and tactical knowledge and skills includes seeking out and implementing best practices as well as exploring and encouraging a culture of sharing among team members to develop and refine their technical proficiency (see table 7-19).

Table 7-19. Demonstrates tactical and technical competence

Strength Indicators	Need Indicators
Uses technical and tactical expertise to accomplish the mission to standard and protect resources.	Uses assets, equipment, procedures, and methods ineffectively.
Displays the appropriate knowledge of methods procedures, and equipment for the position.	Consumes excessive resources due to ineffective use of technology.
Embraces and employs new technology to accomplish the mission.	Uses outdated or ineffective approaches to problems. Uninterested in new knowledge and skills.

Underlying Causes	
Does not have a full awareness of organization positions and operations.	
Does not understand the optimal employment of assets, equipment, procedures, and methods.	
Does not seek opportunities to learn new solutions for technical and tactical problems.	
Is not comfortable with new technology and is unaware of its capabilities.	
Unaware of how to locate and learn new technical and tactical knowledge and skills.	

Feedback	Learn from those around you by asking which skills and what knowledge is mission-critical. Ask others how they learned it, and follow a similar path. Talk with others inside and outside the chain of command to stay current on external influences (such as emerging technology or latest tactics, techniques and procedures). Key opportunities to network and share information include attendance at conferences and training courses, as well as online resources. Look for opportunities to test your technical and tactical proficiency. Self-monitor your ability to be a technical and tactical leader by reading the latest journal articles, professional journals, and professional association releases and comparing personal knowledge and skills to emerging information.
Study	Build personal expertise by reviewing doctrine, technical manuals, and non-military references in areas of interest. Subscribe to or research professional journals and resources dealing with a new technical skill or capability. Keep current on emerging technical information by reviewing blogs and other Web-based resources. Volunteer to prepare and deliver training on a specific technical or tactical subject. Write and submit a journal or magazine article on your technical area of expertise. Look for opportunities to take a continuing studies course to build technical knowledge. Consider resident, distance or distributed learning, and correspondence offerings.
Practice	Find and pursue opportunities for advanced training pertaining to personal responsibilities. Volunteer for opportunities that will provide technical or tactical experience in new areas. Develop one or more specialty area where you will be considered the unit expert. Communicate your knowledge and make yourself available when others need guidance or support.

UNDERSTANDS AND MODELS CONCEPTUAL SKILLS

7-31. Army leaders must not only understand the importance of conceptual skills, they must possess, continually develop, and model them as well (see table 7-20 on page 7-22). Conceptual skills are the basis for making sense of complex situations, understanding cause and effect, critical thinking, solving problems, developing plans, and leading others. In short, they are essential to accomplishing the critical functions of the Army.

Table 7-20. Understands and models conceptual skills

Strength Indicators	Need Indicators
Identifies the critical issues present in a situation or issue and uses this knowledge to make decisions and take advantage of opportunities. Recognizes and generates innovative solutions. Relates and compares information from different sources to identify possible cause-and-effect relationships. Uses sound judgment, logical reasoning, and critical thinking. Makes logical assumptions in the absence of facts.	Gets lost in the details of a situation without perceiving how they fit together and interact. Comfortably maintains the status quo; ignores new thought processes to solve a problem. Overly relies on one source of information or one approach to problem solving. Employs stereotyped, rigid, or biased thinking when making sense of a situation. Uses a scattered approach to thinking through problems and developing solutions. Does not articulate the evidence and thought processes leading to decisions.
Underlying Causes	
Impatient with the time or effort required for rigorous conceptualization. Uses gut instinct or past approaches to make decisions. Fears the risk of failure that may come from new conceptualizations or approaches. Unsure of the thought process and evidence used to reach decisions and unable to articulate them to others. Does not take time for personal reflection and thought.	
Feedback	Ask yourself how an issue and related decisions or actions will fit into the larger view of events. What other decisions, operations, or units are affected? Ask others if they have observed you showing personal biases or conceptual shortcomings during analysis or problem solving. Ask for clear and honest feedback regarding perceived biases and conceptual difficulties. Compare this feedback to a personal self-assessment. Consider the long-term consequences to a decision or action you are contemplating. What are the second- or third-order effects? Identify the consequences and re-evaluate the potential decision. Present the idea to others and request their input.
Study	Read about methods of conceptualizing ambiguous and complex situations. Topics may include systems thinking, mind mapping, and others. Train yourself to visualize how plans or operations will unfold by thinking through branches, phases, sequences, and time schedules. Study the topics of critical and creative thinking; apply the methods to issues you face. Observe a leader who is adept at conceptual skills and developing conceptual models. Discuss the leader's thought process with the leader. Access the Virtual Improvement Center to complete: Leadership Decision Making or Being an Adaptable Leader in Times of Change.
Practice	When faced with a problem, apply a systematic approach to define the problem, gather relevant information, make essential assumptions, and develop courses of action. Work to synthesize facts, data, experiences, and principles to make sense of situations. Look for patterns, themes, connections, and interactions. When faced with a problem, take time to develop multiple plausible solutions to the problem. Apply pre-selected criteria to help evaluate the solutions and select the best. Use a mind mapping technique or tool to make sense of the elements of a complex or ambiguous situation and their relationships. Create and communicate your vision for the outcome of an important effort and the process to achieve the outcome.

SEEKS DIVERSE IDEAS AND POINTS OF VIEW

7-32. By seeking and being open to diverse ideas and points of view, Army leaders become exposed to new ideas, perspectives, explanations, and approaches that can help achieve tasks and projects more efficiently and effectively. Consideration of diverse ideas and points of view helps ensure the adequate conceptualization of issues as well as the development and selection of viable courses of action. Being open to diverse ideas and points of view also aids in the perception of change, identification of new requirements, and adaptability to dynamic operational environments (see table 7-21).

Table 7-21. Seeks diverse ideas and points of view

Strength Indicators	Need Indicators
Encourages respectful, honest communication among staff and decision makers.	Settles for the first solution that comes to mind.
Explores alternative explanations and approaches for accomplishing tasks.	Views subordinates' opinions and ideas as irrelevant.
Reinforces new ideas; Willing to consider alternative perspectives to resolve difficult problems.	Does not express opposing views to gain favor or avoid argument.
Uses knowledgeable sources and subject matter experts.	Operates in isolation.
Encourages team members to express their ideas even if they question the consensus.	Maintains the status quo and hesitates to alter current "tried and true" approaches.
	Belittles, bullies, and berates rather than offering constructive and specific feedback.

Underlying Causes
Views subordinates' ideas as threats to personal expertise or authority.
Impatient with talk and discussion; wants to quickly reach a decision.
Has difficulty perceiving or understanding shades of meaning or differences in opinion.
Relies excessively on certain individuals' perspectives; does not offer everyone a chance for input.
Does not take time for personal reflection and thought.

Feedback	Encourage team members to express ideas and opinions about the team's functioning. Use active listening methods to ensure accurate understanding of their perspectives.
	Get someone skilled in team processes and communications to observe a team meeting and provide feedback on how open to diverse ideas and opinions you appeared to be and how you encouraged or discouraged ideas and opinions.
	Communicate the desired outcome of task and ask team members for their feedback and opinions. Use that opinion to devise new and more effective strategies.
Study	Learn how to conduct research in subject areas important to your position.
	Get involved in your professional community by participating in associations and groups that promote learning and creative solutions.
	Interview a leader with a reputation as a strong innovator and leader of teams that solve complex and unique challenges. Learn about the thought process and methods used to get the best from team members and reach a creative solution.
	Read about the approaches and methods that people in other fields or from other backgrounds used to solve problems like those you face.
	Access the Virtual Improvement Center to complete: Seeking and Incorporating Diverse Ideas; Achieving Shared Understanding; The Art of Asking Questions; Seeking and Delivering Face-to-Face Feedback; Beyond People Skills: Leveraging Your Understanding of Others.
Practice	Keep an open mind even when ideas do not fit conventional thinking or seem to be tangential to the mission.
	Ensure that when team member ideas are 'off target' that you do not belittle or berate them. Look for the merit in every argument rather than the fatal flaw.
	Purposefully assemble diverse teams for projects or tasks. Solicit input and opinion from all team members when trying to find a solution to the problem.
	Do not dismiss others' opinions because of their grade, age, or gender. Actively listen to their opinion and determine how to apply the approach to a particular solution.
	Meet with the team to brainstorm creative solutions to a challenge that the organization or unit currently faces. Try to approach the problem from a new and different direction.

COMMUNICATES

7-33. Leaders communicate by clearly expressing ideas and actively listening to others. By understanding the nature and importance of communication and practicing effective communication techniques, leaders will relate better to others and be able to translate goals into actions.

7-34. Communication is essential to all other leadership competencies. Four components are in this competency:

- Listens actively.
- Creates shared understanding.
- Employs engaging communication techniques.
- Sensitive to cultural factors in communication.

LISTENS ACTIVELY

7-35. The most important purpose of listening is to comprehend the speaker's thoughts and internalize them. Throughout a conversation, listeners should pay attention to what the other is trying to communicate. Active listeners have a lot to focus on—a variety of verbal and nonverbal cues, the content of the message the speaker is trying to deliver, and the urgency and emotion of the speaker (see table 7-22). Stay alert for common themes that recur with the speaker as well as inconsistencies or topics they completely avoid.

Table 7-22. Listens actively

Strength Indicators	Need Indicators
Pays attention to nonverbal cues.	Interrupts to provide own opinions and decisions.
Asks questions to clarify meaning when the speaker's point is not understood.	Distracted by anger or disagreement with the speaker.
Summarizes and paraphrases the speaker's main points before creating an answer.	Uses the first response that comes to mind.
Maintains eye contact.	Focuses attention on taking copious notes.
Takes brief mental or written notes on important points for clarification.	Confuses the overall point of the message with the details provided.
Stays alert for the speaker's common themes.	Tells people what they should say or think.
Reflects on information before expressing views.	

Underlying Causes
Focused on what to say next rather than accurately understanding the other person.
Unskilled at accurately perceiving feelings and reading body language.
Feels uncomfortable with the topic, information, or emotions the speaker is sharing.
Believes that own way is the only way; does not listen to others' opinions.
Distracted by time pressure, other concerns, or environmental factors.

Feedback	If you do not understand what the speaker tries to communicate, ask them to restate the idea.
	Paraphrase what the speaker said before you respond. Use wording such as "So what you're saying is…"
	Ask others, at work or in your network, how you can improve active listening skills.
	At the close of a conversation, recap or summarize the main points and the motivations that might be behind them. Note trends and themes from the discussion.
Study	During daily activities, try to observe someone who you feel is a strong listener interacting with someone else. What makes that person a good listener? What verbal and nonverbal cues are used?
	Learn what behaviors limit active listening. Consider how often you say things such as "Yes, but…" or "Let's get to the point." Do you check your mobile device or continue to type on the computer during conversations? These types of behaviors tend to communicate an unwillingness to listen and limit conversation.
	Find out if you are a selective listener by observing what topics, what people, and in what settings you are or are not an active listener.
	Access the Virtual Improvement Center to complete: Achieving Shared Understanding, The Art of Asking Questions, Building Working Relationships across Boundaries, Seeking and Delivering Face-to-Face Feedback, Navigating Contentious Conversations, Managing Difficult Behavior, Beyond People Skills: Leveraging Your Understanding of Others.

Table 7-22. Listens actively (continued)

Practice	During conversations, offer brief summary statements of the person's statements and associated feelings. Look for confirmation of your understanding from the other person. Paraphrase in your own words to avoid parroting the words of the other person, which they may perceive as mocking. Employ verbal prompts, such as "Yes…", "Go on…", and "Tell me more…" and nonverbal prompts, such as nodding your head, leaning toward the other person, and making eye contact to encourage the other person to talk. During everyday conversations, try to focus solely on what the speaker is saying rather than forming your argument. Minimize external distractions by turning off mobile devices and closing the door or going where you can be with the speaker one-on-one. If this is not convenient, ask to meet the speaker later to focus on what the speaker has to say. Try not to argue mentally with the person. It distracts you from listening to what the speaker is trying to convey. Take notes that identify important points or items for clarification during meetings. Review your notes and follow-up with an email or conversation if it remains unclear.

CREATES SHARED UNDERSTANDING

7-36. Leaders should understand the unit's mission and develop plans to meet mission goals. Leaders owe it to subordinates, the organization, and unified action partners to share information that directly applies to their duties and provides the necessary context for what needs to be done (see table 7-23). Keeping team members informed aligns the organization, relieves stress, and shows appreciation for team members.

Table 7-23. Creates shared understanding

Strength Indicators	Need Indicators
Expresses thoughts and ideas clearly. Double checks that subordinates understand the communicated message. Reinforces the importance of current unit objectives and priorities for subordinates. Recognizes and addresses the potential for miscommunication. Uses a communication method aligned with the information that will be expressed. Communicates to subordinates as well as superiors to ensure everyone is in the loop.	Creates inconsistent and confusing messages, arguments, and stories. Communicates technical subject matter without converting it into general terms. Places an emphasis on the wrong subject matter for an audience (too simplistic for management and too detail-heavy or strategically focused for subordinates). Shares information and understanding with only select favorites. Limits communication to subordinates and superiors in own chain of command.
Underlying Causes	
Has only a little preparation time before speaking to individuals or a group on a topic. Does not have accurate knowledge of the gaps in the audience's understanding of the subject. Not skilled in creating messages or explanations suited to the audience's background, comprehension level, language, culture, or other factors. Partial or incomplete understanding of the subject matter.	
Feedback	Encourage open feedback and dialogue among and with subordinates, particularly when they are asking questions about a project or process. Discuss intent, priorities, and thought processes with subordinates to ensure understanding. Offer subordinates the opportunity to ask about any points they may not have understood. After delivering information, ask others to summarize the information just delivered. Communicate this in a nonthreatening or condescending way but show interest in making sure that everyone is on the same page. Periodically check-in with team members and subordinates to ensure they know what is going on in the organization. Fill them in on any missing details.

Table 7-23. Creates shared understanding (continued)

Study	Assess the best way to communicate with different individuals or groups both inside and outside the organization. Learn how to match the message and method to the audience. Study individuals (public figures, historical, or local) considered skilled communicators and able to provide messages that translated into action. Take a course on effective communications techniques or join a public speaking group to build your knowledge and skill in creating and delivering compelling messages to others. Access the Virtual Improvement Center to complete: Making Influence Count; Achieving Shared Understanding; The Art of Asking Questions; Rapid Team Stand-up: How to Build Your Team ASAP; Building Working Relationships Across Boundaries; Beyond People Skills: Leveraging Your Understanding of Others, Navigating Contentious Conversations; The Leader as Follower. ASAP: as soon as possible
Practice	Relate the unit's current objectives and priorities to the larger organizational goals. As you plan the words and delivery of the message, imagine how the intended audience will receive the message. Consider the information you are trying to explain and build the explanation in a logical progression that fits the topic (such as chronological, sequential, top down, or bottom up). Do not overload the team with information. Offer information in segments for understanding without causing confusion and together will convey the complete story.

EMPLOYS ENGAGING COMMUNICATION TECHNIQUES

7-37. Leaders must deliver a message clearly and succinctly to the unit or subordinates to ensure shared understanding (see table 7-24). To ensure that the message stands out from the crowd, leaders will need to employ engaging communication techniques to make sure the message understood and remembered.

Table 7-24. Employs engaging communication techniques

Strength Indicators	*Need Indicators*
States goals to energize others. Makes eye contact when speaking. Speaks enthusiastically; maintains listeners' interest. Uses appropriate gestures. Selects the appropriate communication medium to deliver the message. Recognizes and addresses misunderstandings. Seeks feedback about how communications worked. Determines, recognizes, and resolves misunderstandings.	Delivers an unclear goal or key message. Provides information using a monotone voice and few aids or devices to support understanding. Uses a condescending tone of voice. Mismatches the message and the communication medium. Takes a long time to express central ideas.
Underlying Causes	
Does not consider the audience well enough; uses words and delivery approach that do not connect. Is not able to communicate the main message succinctly and clearly. Is uncomfortable presenting information to others. Matches a message with an inappropriate communication medium (such as delivering constructive criticism via email rather than face-to-face). Does not have ample time to prepare the information for delivery.	

Table 7-24. Employs engaging communication techniques (continued)

Feedback	Assess the individual or group to see if they are engaged in what you are conveying. Shift the conversation or the method of delivery based on verbal and nonverbal cues. Ask team members or subordinates to give you specific feedback on your ability to deliver information in an engaging and easily comprehensible manner. Ask how to improve. During a presentation or meeting, ask direct and specific questions about the information you are communicating. Talk to team members or subordinates about misunderstandings when they arise. Analyze the reasons why a misunderstanding may have occurred.
Study	Assess the best way to communicate with various individuals in the organization including superiors, peers, and subordinates. Match method with the individual. Measure whether team members are absorbing the thoughts and ideas provided to them. Indicators may include more eye contact, following directions accurately, asking fewer questions for clarification, or appearing more relaxed. Observe someone who seems to connect when communicating with others. Investigate how they generate interest and retain attention. What communication techniques are used? Access the Virtual Improvement Center to complete: Seeking and Delivering Face-to-Face Feedback; Navigating Contentious Conversations.
Practice	Communicate thoughts and ideas in a simple way that all staff understands using a logical and sequential progression. Provide supporting details to prove your central idea. Create buzz around new tasks that the unit is undertaking. Have informal conversations with subordinates about the benefits of the new task. Convey enthusiasm both verbally (using active vice passive words) and nonverbally (with posture, tone, or gestures). Match tone of voice with the information to be delivered. For example, if the unit will undergo a major change, use a direct, clear, and reassuring tone. If the unit is embarking on a new and innovative task, use a tone that builds excitement and enthusiasm. Employ a variety of techniques to ensure that the audience is engaged in the presented information, such as stories, anecdotes, and examples. Use visual aids, when appropriate, to support the message. Make sure that visual aids have a clear and direct relationship to the presented information.

SENSITIVE TO CULTURAL FACTORS IN COMMUNICATION

7-38. Cultural awareness and understanding of how cultural factors can influence the success of communications has long been an important competency for military leaders leading ethnically and culturally diverse organizations. In recent years, the necessities of counterinsurgency, stability, and interorganizational operations have placed cross-cultural communications skills at the center of operational success.

7-39. Understanding cross-cultural factors and the ability to adjust communication attempts to accommodate and capitalize on them are crucial in today's operational environment (see table 7-25). It is important to note that Soldiers do not have to agree with all of the cultural norms or practices; however, they must understand how those cultural values affect interactions with individuals from that culture.

Table 7-25. Sensitive to cultural factors in communication

Strength Indicators	Need Indicators
Is sensitive to cultural variations in communication; is willing to accommodate or adapt to them.	Stereotypes and generalizes about individuals based on their culture, race, or ethnicity.
Maintains a broad awareness of communication customs, expressions, and behaviors.	Avoids situations where interacting with other cultures is required.
Demonstrates respect for others regardless of their culture, race, or ethnicity.	Assumes that individuals from other cultures have the same values, priorities, and worldview as Americans.
Looks beyond individual features or manner of communication to discern the message and its meaning.	Pushes personal beliefs or norms onto an individual from a different culture, race, or ethnicity.

Table 7-25. Sensitive to cultural factors in communication (continued)

	Underlying Causes
	Assumes American views and understanding is correct and other perspectives are less developed or faulty.
	Fears how individuals from different cultures will react to American cultural norms and mores.
	Fears embarrassment; self-conscious about not understanding or violating another culture's norms or mores.
	Believes cultural differences are too great to permit creation of an advantageous alliance.
	Does not have the time or inclination to focus on learning about a new culture.
	Lack of exposure to other cultures or previous negative experience with individuals from other cultures
Feedback	Connect with an individual, with whom you are comfortable, from a different culture to discuss their social norms, mores, and expectations. Obtain feedback on how appropriate or effective your interpersonal communications habits are likely to be with other members of their culture.
	Seek help from external resources (such as chaplains or counselors) for overcoming any deep-seated biases due to traumatic or negative experiences with individuals from other cultures.
	Take advantage of counterinsurgency field exercises to practice culturally appropriate communications skills and receive feedback on their effectiveness.
	Share what you have learned about other cultures with peers and subordinates. Discuss effective and ineffective approaches to cross-cultural communications.
	Seek help (such as chaplains or counselors) if you have any deep-rooted biases or issues that may affect your ability to function effectively in a specific culture.
Study	Become a part of a club or professional association that fosters and encourages cross-cultural understanding. Research opportunities by contacting cultural organizations and asking about cross-cultural meet-ups.
	Take a foreign language or culture course at a community college. Pay attention to specific cultural norms and practices. Highlight areas of cultural difference common across all cultures (such as religion, sport, economic structure, gender difference, or power distance).
	Use resources and references to examine a culture's history, society, religion, sports, governance, lifestyle, business practices, current events, and other important aspects.
	Observe and assess how others with extensive cross-cultural communication experience conduct themselves when communicating across cultures. Look for attitudes, behaviors, and methods that you can adopt.
	Access the Virtual Improvement Center to complete: Making Influence Count; Seeking and Incorporating Diverse Ideas; Building Working Relationships across Boundaries.
Practice	Make a genuine effort to communicate with an individual from another culture by learning and using culturally correct communication, greetings, behaviors, and patterns. Solicit feedback to understand their interpretation of American culture and your behavior.
	Make a personal inventory of your own biases. Create and implement actionable steps to reduce these issues.
	Focus awareness on how you evaluate others and the role cultural differences play. Attempt to evaluate people on an individual basis rather than cultural stereotypes.
	Use active listening techniques, such as summarizing the main points of an individual's discussion to ensure mutual understanding.
	Be on the lookout for possible misunderstanding or misinterpretation. Proactively consider issues from other cultures' perspective.

CREATES A POSITIVE ENVIRONMENT/FOSTERS ESPRIT DE CORPS

7-40. Leaders have the responsibility to establish and maintain appropriate expectations and attitudes that foster healthy relationships and a positive organizational climate. Leaders are charged with improving the organization while accomplishing missions. They should leave the organization better than it was when they arrived. This competency has eight components:

- Fosters teamwork, cohesion, cooperation, and loyalty (esprit de corps).
- Encourages fairness and inclusiveness.

- Encourages open and candid communications.
- Creates a learning environment.
- Encourages subordinates to exercise initiative, accept responsibility, and take ownership.
- Demonstrates care for follower well-being.
- Anticipates people's on-duty needs.
- Sets and maintains high expectations for individuals and teams.

FOSTERS TEAMWORK, COHESION, COOPERATION, AND LOYALTY (ESPRIT DE CORPS)

7-41. A team is a group of individuals with complementary skills committed to a common purpose, set of performance goals, and approach for which they hold themselves mutually accountable. Commitment may not always be present from the start, but it is critical for team sustainability. The team needs to have a detailed common purpose so that all members can understand the what, how, and who (see table 7-26).

Table 7-26. Fosters teamwork, cohesion, cooperation, and loyalty

Strength Indicators	Need Indicators
Encourages people to work together effectively.	Attributes mission success or failure to the performance of individuals.
Promotes teamwork and achievement to build trust.	
Draws attention to the consequences of poor coordination.	Regularly provides meaningful assignments to high-performing or experienced team members over new or less experienced team members.
Attributes mission success or failure to team performance.	
Rapidly and effectively integrates new members.	Maximizes the skills and talents of only a few team members.
Uses unit activities to build cohesion and trust.	
Encourages team members to take on extra responsibilities for the betterment of the unit.	Permits team members to take independent approaches to accomplishing unit tasks.
Maximizes talents of all members of the team.	

Underlying Causes	
Places greater importance on individual contribution than team-based contribution.	
Manages a group that prefers to work individually rather than as a team.	
Feels less comfortable guiding a team than guiding individuals.	
Lacks a clear process for integrating new members and making them feel like they are part the team.	
Lacks awareness of the talents and capabilities of team members.	
Lacks trust in capabilities and dependability of team members.	

Feedback	Use reviews to share feedback and promote unit and team self-improvement. Share ways that the team could improve as a whole rather than singling out individuals.
	Articulate the strengths, limitations, preferences, and beliefs of the team members to superiors. Act as an advocate to promote unit interests and needs.
	Seek feedback on how you work with team members and subordinates in a way that promotes accomplishment of the organization's mission, and how you provide purpose, direction, and motivation to team members.
	Self-assess your ability to manage the team. How do you facilitate teamwork and cohesion? Do you support and guide team members through difficult situations?
Study	Set aside time to become familiar with subordinates' career goals. Ask subordinates questions that treat them as individuals who you want to see succeed.
	Identify and utilize informal and formal unit leaders, such as an individual team members respect and admire. Examine why others view this individual as a role model and seek ways to use this to build cohesion and teamwork.
	Solicit recommended reading or documents on team building from trusted mentors and from content experts within the Army.
	Identify and develop clear linkages between team training and higher unit missions and success.
	Access the Virtual Improvement Center to complete: Rapid Team Stand-up: How to Build Your Team ASAP, Building Trust, and Fostering Team Unity.
	ASAP: as soon as possible

Table 7-26. Fosters teamwork, cohesion, cooperation, and loyalty (continued)

Practice	Define and gain agreement on team missions, standards, and expectations. Have all team members participate in this process so they buy into what is developed. Identify and address internal conflicts to minimize effects on team productivity and morale. Identify and determine opportunities to highlight team interdependencies. Illustrate how an ability to perform in the position successfully depends on the performance of others. Acknowledge and celebrate team accomplishments to build cohesion. Define success by team accomplishment rather than individual achievement. Make a point of welcoming and transitioning new team members by ensuring their first few weeks go smoothly. Assign them a mentor or buddy; speak with them periodically. Promote teamwork across units and discourages us-versus-them thinking and behaviors. Reinforce and promote a sense of identity and pride among team members.

ENCOURAGES FAIRNESS AND INCLUSIVENESS

7-42. To build a positive climate, leaders should use consistent but flexible policies and viewpoints in personally treating others with respect (see table 7-27). While leaders should treat all team members fairly and consistently, not everyone will be treated exactly the same since not all have the same strengths or needs. Fairness means that no one gets preferential treatment, but leaves leeway for team member capabilities and needs. Inclusiveness means that all are valued and accepted into the organization, regardless of differences.

Table 7-27. Encourages fairness and inclusiveness

Strength Indicators	*Need Indicators*
Applies the same guidance, requirements, and policies to all team members and subordinates in the organization. Uses skills and capabilities of team members without providing preferential treatment. Adheres to equal opportunity policies and prevents harassment. Encourages and supports diversity and inclusiveness. Actively seeks to integrate all team members and subordinates into the unit. Encourages learning about and leveraging diversity.	Exempts a select few team members or subordinates from duties. Selects the same high-performing members for almost all developmental opportunities. Prevents high-performers from attending developmental opportunities (such as resident training or education) because of their value to the unit mission. Grants permission for training and professional development only for developmental needs. Allows groups or teams to isolate individuals they do not like or have difficulty fitting in. Saddles burden on high performers.
	*Underlying Causes*
	Gravitates to certain team members and wants to provide them with opportunities for development. Does not successfully balance the need to develop Soldiers with the need to accomplish the mission. Uses favoritism as a tool to retain team members and subordinates. Trusts high performers to produce results with limited oversight and guidance. Does not realize that team members or subordinates are isolating select members of the team. Conducts an incomplete assessment of the capabilities of some groups or individuals.

Feedback	Dedicate time during the duty day to meet subordinates one-on-one to ask about their feelings regarding fairness in the unit. Do they believe only a select few get opportunities? Are some given tasks that lead to more development than others? If a team member says you are unfair, ask about their feelings. Let them speak their mind. Reflect upon what they said and ask yourself if their views have merit. Seek out a trusted peer or subordinate to solicit their input regarding your potential lack of fairness. Consult with a trusted subordinate to discover biases that unit members may hold toward others based on their character, personality, religion, race, ethnicity, or culture. Discuss the biases and devise strategies to overcome them.

Table 7-27. Encourages fairness and inclusiveness (continued)

Study	Create an action plan with specific tactics detailing how to make the unit more fair and inclusive. Document progress towards these goals on a monthly basis.
	Set aside time to familiarize yourself with policies related to equal opportunity and harassment that outline team members and subordinates' responsibilities.
	Apply guidance, requirements, and policies to the roles and responsibilities of each team member. Document how you applied the policy or guidance on a piece of paper in case you need to reference or communicate it later to someone else.
	Participate in a training course or read reference material on how to create an inclusive environment. Document how specific information pertains to the organization.
	Reflect upon your record of selecting subordinates for developmental assignments and opportunities (including approving and sending subordinates to resident training and education). Was your approach fair?
	Access the Virtual Improvement Center to complete: Seeking and Incorporating Diverse Ideas; Building Trust.
Practice	Lead by example by treating others the way you want to be treated. Favoritism makes team members feel that they are not important contributors. Invest time and effort in all members to develop them.
	Create a succession plan for key positions in your organization. Develop a pool of individuals who could fill the positions in case some do not work as you hoped.
	Inclusiveness starts with the members already in the environment. Directly challenge unit obstacles to inclusiveness. Does the unit have certain individuals who do not mesh well with the group? What prevents them from successfully fitting-in with the group?

ENCOURAGES OPEN AND CANDID COMMUNICATIONS

7-43. Good leaders should encourage collaboration through open and candid communications to create an environment where others feel free to contribute and know that their ideas and input are valued. Creating an open environment is a key to developing a unit capable of reacting to change. Leaders that value and reinforce open and candid communications, should show respect for subordinate opinions, recognize others' viewpoints, and encourage input and feedback (see table 7-28).

Table 7-28. Encourages open and candid communications

Strength Indicators	Need Indicators
Reinforces the importance of expressing contrary and minority viewpoints to guard against groupthink.	Demeans team member and subordinate opinions either consciously or subconsciously.
Remains calm, objective, and facts-focused when receiving potentially bad news.	Halts conversation when it appears to be moving towards a change in unit processes or practices.
Encourages input and feedback especially during times of change.	Reacts viscerally or angrily when receiving bad news or conflicting information.
Shows respect for subordinate opinions even while disagreeing with them.	Shares information and understanding with only select favorites who disseminate information to the rest of the unit.
Communicates positive attitude to encourage others and improve morale.	
Displays appropriate reactions to new or conflicting information or opinions.	
Guards against groupthink.	
Underlying Causes	
Concerned that too much open communication can lead to "too much talking and not enough doing."	
Wants to stay true to the current direction of the unit provided by superiors.	
Has too many simultaneous tasks moving forward to take time to hear others' ideas.	
Does not fully understand the relationship between an open environment and adapting to change.	
Has difficulty adapting (emotionally or cognitively) to unforeseen problems, bad news, or conflicting information.	
Feels the need to control information.	

Table 7-28. Encourages open and candid communications (continued)

Feedback	Hold monthly updates where members share information and provide status on tasks.
	Hold a brainstorming session or forum with team members to discuss possible solutions to obstacles currently impeding progress. Ask for opinions on how to remove the obstacle.
	Hold regular unit meetings to discuss internal operations and ongoing issues. Stress taking initiative, underwriting honest mistakes, and continuous improvement.
	Ensure team members feel comfortable presenting their thoughts and ideas. If they are uncomfortable communicating their ideas, hold one-on-one conversations to seek their feedback and input into the process.
	Lead by example. Ask for feedback from team members and subordinates on your ideas. If they come up with a good idea or insight, incorporate it into a new initiative.
Study	Observe a leader whose unit has an open communications environment. Watch what the leader does, and incorporate ideas into personal practices.
	Take a course on soliciting input and open communications. Make sure the course has hands-on examples and scenarios so you can practice improving your skills.
	Reflect upon your communication style with others (including superiors, team members, and subordinates). Is it conducive to the open and candid flow of information and ideas? Note things to improve and incorporate these changes into future communications.
	Research how to foster an open communications environment.
	Access the Virtual Improvement Center to complete: Seeking and Incorporating Diverse Ideas; Navigating Contentious Conversations; Seeking and Delivering Face-to-Face Feedback; The Leader as Follower.
Practice	Make an effort to know superiors, peers, and subordinates. Showing interest lets them know they are valued as unit members beyond the work they produce.
	Show team members that their ideas are valued and are an important part of unit success.
	Demonstrate results by empowering team members and subordinates when they develop a good idea. Communicate that their idea was so strong that the unit will implement it.
	Recognize team members and subordinates for a job well done at meetings or events.
	Conduct regular informal discussions with Soldiers to solicit their ideas for how to address problems and improve processes. Guide the conversation to reinforce and cultivate opinions or views that may differ from typical responses.

CREATES A LEARNING ENVIRONMENT

7-44. The Army seeks to constantly reinvigorate and renew its processes to more efficiently and effectively accomplish its strategic mission. To do so, it depends on the experiences of its people and organizations to contribute to a climate that values and supports learning. By both acknowledging and embracing the importance of learning, leaders actively foster both a culture dedicated to life-long learning and a cadre of leaders who possess a thirst for knowledge and innovation (see table 7-29).

Table 7-29. Creates a learning environment

Strength Indicators	Need Indicators
Uses effective assessment and training methods.	Puts the onus on other leaders to take full responsibility for the development of their subordinates.
Challenges how the organization operates, especially those processes only done in a certain manner "because they've always been done that way."	Adopts a "go at it alone" mentality, and fosters an individualistic unit climate.
Discards techniques or procedures that have outlived their purpose.	Requires that others follow the rules, allowing no room for deviation or innovation.
Regularly expresses the value of seeking counsel and expert advice.	Holds on to techniques or procedures, regardless of their utility, efficiency, or effectiveness.
Encourages leaders and their subordinates to reach their full potential.	Accepts outcomes as they are and moves on to the next task.
Motivates and stimulates innovative and critical thinking in others.	Fails to seek advice or counsel when facing a new or complex task.
Seeks new approaches to problems.	

Table 7-29. Creates a learning environment (continued)

		Underlying Causes
		Unaware of or unwilling to improve the effectiveness of assessment and training methods.

	Underlying Causes
	Unaware of or unwilling to improve the effectiveness of assessment and training methods.
	Believes that no matter what example is set, subordinates will not seek self-development opportunities.
	Feels that rules and procedures were put in place to be followed.
	Supporter of traditional values and approaches to problems.
	Afraid of change and the possible difficulties and turmoil that accompany new techniques or procedures.
	Feels that effective leaders are "take charge" and are "decision makers." Seeking advice or counsel is a sign of weakness and lack of expertise.
Feedback	Informally ask unit members why processes are done certain ways. Identify processes that appear to be performed a certain way for no apparent reason other than they have always been done that way. Brainstorm ways to improve these processes. Make a habit of asking yourself why you perform processes or activities a certain way. If the best answer you have is "because I've always done it that way," reconsider your approach. Ask unit members about processes that frustrate them. Encourage them to think of a more effective way. Show that you value their feedback by incorporating their suggestions, as appropriate. Have a conversation with your superior about the unit environment. Ask if they feel that it currently supports learning or if there are ways that it could be more supportive. Gather lessons learned from recent tasks to improve their execution in the future.
Study	Ask other unit leaders what assessment and training techniques they are using. Document these techniques and evaluate which ones would work best. Understand how the Army officially defines "life-long learning". Think about what that means for you, the unit, and the Army organization as a whole. Think about great Army leaders who inspire you. Highlight any of their actions that helped to advance the Army as a "learning organization." Use these actions to spur insights that may be able to relate or incorporate with the unit. Choose one unit process to study. Document exactly how it occurs, from start to finish. Identify areas where the process may hit obstacles. Brainstorm possible solutions to either overcome the obstacles or circumvent them. Access the Virtual Improvement Center to complete: The Leader's Role in Providing On-the-Job Learning and Support; Supporting the Developing Leader; Counseling and Coaching Videos.
Practice	Conduct periodic brainstorming sessions with groups of subordinates to think through likely problems the unit may face. Guide the discussion as an opportunity to reinforce the idea of creative sharing and the importance of others' advice and counsel. While performing normal duties, identify processes or procedures that seem slow or inefficient. Identify and incorporate new methods to increase efficiency. Set a self-development example by sharing opportunities related to developmental activities or training. Share your experience with team members. During the next unit briefing, consciously make an effort to include information about the importance of interacting with others and seeking counsel. Couch it in the context of the Army's organization-wide commitment to life-long learning.

ENCOURAGES SUBORDINATES TO EXERCISE INITIATIVE, ACCEPT RESPONSIBILITY, AND TAKE OWNERSHIP

7-45. As a leader, one of the greatest challenges is to encourage subordinates to exercise initiative, accept responsibility, and take ownership. Subordinates may hesitate to step forward and express their technical knowledge or provide information because they fear hearing they are wrong or do not want to take on an additional task. It is a leader's responsibility to build confidence in a subordinate's ability to solve problems, set the conditions that foster taking initiative, and encourage input from anyone with an understanding of the applicable subject matter (see table 7-30).

Table 7-30. Encourages subordinates

Strength Indicators	Need Indicators
Encourages subordinates to explore new approaches to a problem.	Hesitates to consider or incorporate subordinates' suggestions into Army unit tasks.
Pushes decision making to the lowest appropriate level to encourage subordinate responsibility and empowerment.	Defines the course for most tasks without consulting team members or experienced subordinates.
Involves others in decisions and keeps them informed of consequences that affect them.	Uses only tried and true approaches to solving problems or completing tasks.
Provides subordinates with their "own piece of the task" to ensure ownership and accountability.	Uses only the same small cadre of team members to support decisionmaking.
Guides team members and subordinates in thinking through problems for themselves.	Takes time to inform a subordinate on how to perform all aspects of a specific task.
Reinforces and rewards initiative.	Treats Soldiers' honest mistakes as things to avoid or prevent—not as opportunities to learn.

Underlying Causes
Satisfied with the status quo; does not seek to improve the unit.
Feels a lack of control when decisionmaking authority is delegated to subordinates.
Has insufficient time to help subordinates think through problems.
Has trouble trusting the judgment abilities of others.
Feels that subordinates are not stepping up to take on new opportunities and challenges.
Feels that mission success is compromised when decisionmaking is delegated to lower levels.

Feedback	When presented with a new task, interview a handful of team members interested in the role. Select the best candidate.
	At the beginning of a new task, hold a brainstorming session with team members to discuss possible solutions to obstacles currently impeding progress. Ask for opinions on how to remove obstacles.
	Hold regular unit meetings to discuss internal operations and ongoing issues. Stress taking initiative, underwriting honest mistakes, and continuous improvement.
	Periodically check-in with team members to ensure they are comfortable with their current task responsibilities. Ensure they do not feel overwhelmed making critical decisions.
Study	Take a course or training on delegation and implement learned techniques on-duty.
	Consult a coach or mentor to discuss your delegating skills. Create a list of tangible practices that you can incorporate on-duty.
	Observe a peer or superior who is adept at delegating responsibility to subordinates. Examine their process for selecting subordinates and communicating responsibility and expectations.
	Allocate time to create an initiatives wish list that you as a leader would like to take on. Share the list with team members and subordinates and discuss how to make wish list items a reality.
	Read a reference book or article to learn about effectively encouraging subordinates to exercise initiative, accept responsibility, and take ownership.
	Access the Virtual Improvement Center to complete: Supporting the Developing Leader; Creating and Supporting Challenging Job Assignments; Enabling Subordinates Using Mission-Focused Delegation.
Practice	Use teams with diverse backgrounds and experience to attack new or complex problems and operations. Encourage trial and error for solutions that are not obvious.
	Delegate stretch assignments to subordinates. Match the complexity of the task to the skill-level and potential of each person.
	Monitor delegated tasks, but do not micromanage. Use progress-related milestones or reviews to ensure progress. Encourage subordinates to ask questions and discuss challenges.
	Have subordinates define what taking initiative and ownership mean to them. Discuss their responses one-on-one and create or provide opportunities to help them develop.
	Conduct periodic brainstorming sessions with subordinates to analyze likely problems the unit may face; guide the discussion as Soldiers think through problems and identify potential obstacles to taking initiative. Use this information to cultivate initiative and ownership.

DEMONSTRATES CARE FOR FOLLOWER WELL-BEING

7-46. Army leaders should cultivate both physical and mental health by being both logical and clear-headed when making decisions. Leaders who emphasize mental and physical health and well-being inspire confidence in subordinates and set an example of how to balance the inherent stresses of both personal and professional life (see table 7-31). Reducing stress and improving physical fitness are excellent tactics for avoiding sickness, promoting mental clarity, and encouraging similar behavior in subordinates.

Table 7-31. Demonstrates care for follower well-being

Strength Indicators	Need Indicators
Ensures subordinates' and their families' health, welfare, and development are provided for.	Unwilling to decline taskings even when the unit is overburdened or at the breaking point.
Monitors morale and encourages honest feedback.	Fails to provide for family and individual support needs.
Sets a personal example for colleagues.	
Nurtures long-term well-being through rigorous training and preparation.	Takes credit for unit success or unfairly blames subordinates when failures are experienced.
Understands and nurtures individual subordinates' intrinsic motivators.	Ignores morale indicators and promotes overly optimistic feedback.
Tells a subordinate to go home when they have been working long hours.	Does not share in the hardships experienced by Soldiers.
Gives subordinate time off during the workday to take care of family matters.	Coddles subordinates with easy or comfortable training.

Underlying Causes	
Wishes to avoid controversial or critical decision-making.	
Wants to please, impress, and create a positive impression to superiors (such as not declining taskings).	
Focused on accomplishing the short-term mission without sufficient concern for the long-term needs and well-being of Soldiers and their families.	
Expects more of subordinates than of oneself.	
Prizes personal relationships over the health, welfare, and safety of the organization.	
Expects that subordinates will be self-sufficient or capable of addressing issues independently.	

Feedback	Encourage peers and subordinates to share their candid opinions, reiterating that you welcome different perspectives.
	Speak with the team and their families to determine how you can better serve them.
	Solicit feedback on specific issues that may be affecting morale. Seek assistance from subordinates in developing a full understanding of the issues.
	Ask subordinates to explain the range of perspectives on an issue rather than only providing their opinions.
	Discuss with the team how to improve training exercises to meet specific objectives.
	Seek feedback from trusted senior subordinates regarding their perceptions of unit welfare and morale—including families. Identify potential stressors or factors negatively affecting the unit and work with subordinates to identify ways to address them.
Study	Observe the behaviors of other leaders who you admire. Note how these leaders make difficult decisions that balance the welfare of Soldiers with mission accomplishment.
	In addition to maintaining personal knowledge and awareness of Army programs, identify and investigate programs offered by local communities and social service organizations that may be of help to Soldiers and their families.
	Regularly reflect upon your actions to balance the welfare of Soldiers and their families with mission accomplishment. When your actions fail to maintain this balance, reflect upon what motivated you to act as you did.
	Question the value of training exercises. Are they rigorous for rigor's sake or do they serve a specific objective, such as safer or more efficient operations?
	Access the Virtual Improvement Center to complete: Seeking and Delivering Face-to-Face Feedback.

Table 7-31. Demonstrates care for follower well-being (continued)

Practice	Set aside social time with subordinates, peers, and their families. These activities can help develop compassion and provide insight for ways to help meet their needs. Draft a statement of how you want the unit to be treated. When the unit's treatment does not live up to your standards, list objectives for improvement to implement. Create a record of each time you rebuke a peer or subordinate for failing to live up to set standards. In the record, include a memory of when you failed to meet the same standard. Ask subordinates and peers to explain their understanding of the reasons for specific training exercises. If they understand the links among training, safety, and effectiveness, they will likely respect the rigor of their training.

ANTICIPATES PEOPLE'S DUTY NEEDS

7-47. To anticipate team member and subordinate on-duty needs, leaders should be aware of each individual's responsibilities, duties, strengths, current workload, as well as their professional interests and goals (see table 7-32). In addition, leaders should become aware of subordinate strengths and developmental needs to provide a holistic understanding of both where the individual currently is and where they want to be. Attempt to match subordinates with tasks and opportunities that not only foster career and professional development, but that also align with their interests and motivations.

Table 7-32. Anticipates people's duty needs

Strength Indicators	*Need Indicators*
Monitors subordinate's current positions, duties, strengths, and developmental needs for a performance baseline. As part of formal counseling sessions or informal conversations with subordinates, discusses and verifies professional interests and goals. Interacts with subordinates frequently to ensure roles and responsibilities are clear and satisfaction and morale are high. Assigns roles based on members' interests, motivation, strengths, and developmental needs against mission tasks.	Does not attempt to account for team member and subordinate developmental needs, professional interests, satisfaction, or morale in assigning positions or tasks. Resources projects without a clear commitment to meet expectations within the required time. Interacts with and observes staff infrequently. Just does it and does not analyze the mission and risk.
Underlying Causes	
Assumes individuals have the same interests and motivators. Allocates insufficient time to become aware of subordinates' professional interests, motivation, strengths, and developmental needs. Believes the role of a leader is to tell people what to do without telling them why. Overly focused on placing the mission first. Does not consider individual and unit morale when assigning individual and unit tasks.	
Feedback	Set aside time to ask subordinates to discuss their position responsibilities. Ensure their understanding of their responsibilities is the same as yours. Reconcile any differences through conversations with the subordinate. Conduct periodic meetings with trusted staff to discuss and gather feedback regarding unit morale and ways to better anticipate the on-duty needs of unit staff. Conduct debriefs after mission completion to compare the performance with the indicators of success and failure, discuss learning opportunities, and focus on problem-solving regarding any mistakes made. Have periodic discussions with subordinates to discuss their current positions, duties, and professional interests and goals, and how well their current duties are aligned with their professional goals.

Table 7-32. Anticipates people's duty needs (continued)

Study	Assess current positions against the mission to identify tasks, knowledge, skills, and abilities the mission requires and are likely to develop.
	Determine whether any additional support will be needed, such as resources, a mentor, or extra time to complete the task.
	Identify and provide resources to team members and subordinates, such as aids and decision support tools, to help make task achievement easier and more stress-free.
	During normal operations, observe team members and subordinates performing their duties to gauge motivation and morale levels as they perform their duties.
	Access the Virtual Improvement Center to complete: The Leader's Role in Providing On-the-Job Learning and Support or Out of Time: Managing Competing Demands.
Practice	Assign roles only after considering the unit member's strengths, developmental needs, and professional interests against mission tasks. Assign challenging roles that will help with growth, development, and gaining confidence in their skills.
	Communicate expectations to unit members about tasks. Be upfront about intentions of why this is a learning opportunity.
	Create opportunities for on-duty learning by pairing team experts with novices.
	Weigh the criticality and time available to accomplish tasks. Time permitting, adjust the pace and personnel involved to balance individual development with meeting objectives.

SETS AND MAINTAINS HIGH EXPECTATIONS FOR INDIVIDUALS AND TEAMS

7-48. Leaders sometimes focus considerable energy on annual performance reviews and do not give sufficient attention to providing guidance and establishing expectations during the course of a rating period.

7-49. Providing direction and setting expectations are crucial to getting the best results and promoting professional and career development. When setting expectations with team members and subordinates, make sure that stated expectations are connected to unit objectives and mission, clearly expressed, and mutually agreed upon (see table 7-33).

Table 7-33. Sets and maintains high expectations for individuals and teams

Strength Indicators	Need Indicators
Clearly articulates expectations for subordinates and teams.	Only sets expectations once per year during the subordinate's performance review.
Expects good performance and does not accept poor performance.	Speaks infrequently with team members regarding how they meet expectations and standards.
Provides recognition of superior performance.	Determines expectations for subordinates without discussion or consultation.
Identifies poor performance and attempts to understand and address its cause.	Does not communicate individual and team expectations.
Speaks frequently with the individual or unit regarding their ability to meet the standard.	Provides expectations to subordinates or teams during the task rather than at the beginning.
Ensures that expectations relate clearly to unit goals, objectives, and mission.	
Underlying Causes	
Feels uncomfortable discussing areas for improvement and delivering feedback.	
Is unclear what expectations for team members and subordinates at different levels should look like.	
Has not allocated appropriate time to speaking with individuals or teams regarding expectations.	
Believes the unit leader should articulate expectations to unit members rather than obtaining acceptance and buy-in from unit members regarding the expectations.	
Does not clearly understand how expectations of subordinates and teams relate to the unit's mission.	

Table 7-33. Sets and maintains high expectations for individuals and teams (continued)

Feedback	Have a peer review the performance expectations you developed for subordinates or team leaders. Tell them to review the document with a critical eye to ensure that it is reasonable given the current environment of the Army.
	Discuss unit expectations and assign stretch tasks to willing individuals or teams. When assigning the tasks, ensure the individuals can visualize how to achieve the goals. If they cannot visualize how to achieve the goals, they will not be able to define a path forward.
	Periodically assess how the measurement of performance expectations is going. Ensure that the data and measures accurately assess performance against expectations.
Study	Study other organizations' performance expectations in the military, public, and private sectors and develop a list of best practices based on what you learned.
	Ensure that you have a firm understanding of the organization's mission and goals. Also, ensure that you understand and can discuss the unit's mission and goals. This should function as a refresher for you to make sure you are on the right page.
	Examine if the unit has a process for goal setting, evaluation, feedback, and accountability that lets team members and subordinates know how they are doing.
	Research how to develop clear, challenging, and achievable goals; discuss with unit members.
	Access the Virtual Improvement Center to complete: Creating and Supporting Challenging Job Assignments; Creating and Promulgating a Vision of the Future.
Practice	Develop expectations for subordinates together. This should not be a management-only task.
	Develop useful measures for performance expectations agreed upon by the entire team. Measures should be consistent for all subordinates and teams and should assess capabilities related to the task.
	Encourage team members and subordinates to stretch themselves to reach for new goals during their performance review. Ask yourself how you know it is a stretch.
	Make sure that definitions of the performance expectations are clear and not open to interpretation. Remember to make them specific and write them down.
	Develop a clear rewards and recognition system. Recognition should communicate the expectations from team members and subordinates for behaviors and conduct.

PREPARES SELF

7-50. Leaders ensure they are prepared to execute their leadership responsibilities fully. They are aware of their limitations and strengths and seek to develop themselves. Leaders maintain physical fitness and mental well-being. They continue to improve the domain knowledge required of their leadership roles and their profession. Only through continuous preparation for missions and other challenges, being aware of self and situations, and practicing life-long learning and development can an individual fulfill the responsibilities of leadership. This competency has seven components:

- Maintains mental and physical health and well-being.
- Expands knowledge of technical, technological, and tactical areas.
- Expands conceptual and interpersonal capabilities.
- Analyzes and organizes information to create knowledge.
- Maintains relevant cultural awareness.
- Maintains relevant geopolitical awareness.
- Maintains self-awareness: employs self-understanding and recognizes effect on others.

MAINTAINS MENTAL AND PHYSICAL HEALTH AND WELL-BEING

7-51. Army leaders cultivate comprehensive fitness through both physical and mental health and make logical and clear-headed decisions (see table 7-34). They inspire confidence in their followers and set the example of how to balance the inherent stresses of both personal and professional life. Reducing stress and improving physical fitness are tactics for avoiding sickness, promoting mental clarity, and encouraging similar outcomes in others.

Table 7-34. Maintains mental and physical health and well-being

Strength Indicators	Need Indicators
Recognizes imbalance or inappropriateness of personal actions. Removes emotions from decisionmaking. Seeks work and life balance. Applies logic and reason to make decisions when interacting with emotionally-charged individuals. Recognizes the sources of stress and maintains appropriate levels of challenge to motivate self. Takes part in regular exercise, leisure activities, and time away from routine work. Stays focused on life priorities and values.	Avoids physical activity. Frequently abandons sleep for other activities. Perpetuates a deadline-based environment that leaves no time for relaxation. Engages in unhealthy eating or drinking habits. Uses tobacco products or misuses legal or illegal drugs or other substances. Allows personal emotions to drive decisions or guide responses to emotionally charged situations. Tries to deny, ignore, or push through stress.

Underlying Causes	
Overwhelmed by workload or responsibility. Poor time management. Keeps emotions contained and does not find opportunities to release them. Lack of experience in new position tasks. Believes that being a Soldier or leader means being able to endure or be immune to high stress levels.	

Feedback	Get periodic health examinations to assess indicators of physical health and stress, as well as lifestyle factors that may affect physical and mental health. Obtain guidance on corrective actions from healthcare and diet professionals. Ask a trusted leader for feedback on your performance in handling emotionally-charged issues or decisions. Are you able to remain logical and objective, or do emotions drive decisions? How might you handle these situations better? Use a trusted family member or friend as an advisor for feedback on your perception and interpretation of events as well as your plans and intended actions.
Study	Observe the behaviors of other leaders you admire. How do they handle their stress? Make a list of the methods they use that you would like to try. Reflect on an incident where stress disrupted your performance. How could you have dealt with the stress better? Consider a high-pressure incident that you handled well. What allowed you to deal effectively with the stress? Analyze your diet by keeping a dietary journal over a one-week period. Identify unhealthy foods (such as high fat, salt, or calories) and healthier alternatives to adopt. Reflect on values and priorities to build a clear sense of direction and perspective. Access the Virtual Improvement Center to complete: The Value of Self-Awareness
Practice	Exercise for 30 minutes or more several times per week. Make aerobic exercise or sport a main component of personal exercise to maintain cardiovascular health and reduce stress. Maintain interest by including favorite sports, exercise with friends, and variety. Make time every day to organize personal activities. Use lists to prioritize what to do, track progress, identify accomplishments, and practice time management. Socialize with others, and maintain friendships. Find a trusted family member or friend to serve as an advisor, someone with whom you can discuss concerns and issues. Reduce or eliminate alcohol and tobacco consumption.

EXPANDS KNOWLEDGE OF TECHNICAL, TECHNOLOGICAL, AND TACTICAL AREAS

7-52. Technical knowledge consists of specialized understanding of a particular function or system. Army leaders are responsible for leveraging both individual and collective specialized knowledge to complete the mission. They must expand their skills in technical, technological, and tactical areas. This requires an understanding of how functional components relate as well as the requirements for training and logistical planning to support technical operations. Army leaders capitalize on opportunities to share knowledge across an organization, especially to use their subordinate's knowledge to educate others on technical and tactical details (see table 7-35). Army leaders also must maintain awareness of new trends and emerging technologies that are available and their application.

Table 7-35. Expands knowledge of technical, technological, and tactical areas

Strength Indicators	Need Indicators
Seeks knowledge of systems, equipment, capabilities, and situations, particularly information technology systems. Encourages understanding of systems. Considers how systems affect doctrine, tactics, organizational design, training, related material, personnel, and facilities. Embraces efforts that share knowledge across and between organizations. Encourages subordinates to share their specialized skills and knowledge. Adapts to new technologies, learning capabilities and shortcomings technical systems offer.	Does not locate and attend to information on new trends, developments, ideas, and technologies that are relevant to or provide context for organizational requirements. Views equipment and technologies in isolation without understanding how they integrate or combine to operate as a system. Sees no personal need to understand technology and technological developments. Hinders the exchange of knowledge between personnel in the organization. Overemphasizes or relies on a single tactic or technical approach that has worked in the past.

Underlying Causes	
View technologies only as their individual components; not practiced in systems thinking. Tries to avoid time and expense required to share or grow technical or tactical knowledge. Is not comfortable with team changes brought on by knowledge sharing and innovation. Is dubious about piloting new technologies or standards. Comfortable with status quo; hesitant to change a proven process or system.	

Feedback	Seek testing and certification in relevant technologies and apply technological competencies. Practice tactics and technologies to address organizational requirements or mission. After each significant attempt, capture the lessons of the experience to guide future attempts. Request that technical staff provide their suggestions on operational and planning details. Request that other technical teams provide updates on their progress and challenges to identify areas that might be able to build collaboration.
Study	Read or engage in technical discussions to understand how components and processes combine to create systems and how to optimally design and employ these systems. Attend briefings, meetings, or courses that address pertinent technologies including the effective uses and limitations of those technologies. Capitalize on opportunities to share technical or tactical information with your team. Run a professional development interest group or forum that focuses on exchanging information and keeping up to date on technical and tactical developments. Engage in a professional reading program that includes books and journals that report on tactical and technological developments and their employment to address operational requirements.
Practice	Employ technologies, organization, people, and processes as an integrated system to produce desired outcomes. List technological knowledge and skills key to individual performance and the functioning of the organization. Implement a method for acquiring and disseminating information about developments in these areas. Organize a session among technical staff from the organization or across similar organizations to share ideas and knowledge. List pros and cons of new technologies or tactics to reason out effects of a new system. Look for ways to test new ideas and technologies in organization operations; incorporate effective innovations into the organization's business processes. This approach supports the goal of continuous organizational improvement.

EXPANDS CONCEPTUAL AND INTERPERSONAL CAPABILITIES

7-53. Conceptual abilities enable sound judgment; help Army leaders think creatively; and permit leaders to reason analytically, critically, ethically, and with cultural sensitivity. Army leaders consider intended and unintended consequences and anticipate the results and consequences of important decisions on people and mission. To expand conceptual and interpersonal capabilities, Army leaders use opportunities to improve reasoning and problem-solving skills and to implement the best solution for the unit (see table 7-36).

Table 7-36. Expands conceptual and interpersonal capabilities

Strength Indicators	Need Indicators
Applies lessons learned to avoid repeating mistakes and guide future actions. Filters unnecessary information efficiently. Sets aside time for self-development, reflection, and personal growth. Understands and appropriately employs critical thinking, imagination, and problem solving under different task conditions. Learns new approaches to problem solving.	Uses limited approaches to problem solving. Accepts problem situations at face value; does not examine them critically or fully; ignores system influences and interactions. Goes with the first solution that might work even if time permits thorough solution development. Becomes overwhelmed and frustrated by the number of details of a situation. Uses a scattered approach to thinking through problems and developing solutions.

Underlying Causes	
Perceived lack of interest or time to learn or engage in critical and creative thinking and problem solving. Fears the risk of failure when opportunities to be innovative present themselves. Does not see the benefit of personal reflection and thought. Perceives a lack of time for self-development, reflection, and personal growth. Is dubious about piloting new ideas or approaches to solving problems.	

Feedback	As you lead a team in complex problem solving, use a skilled problem solver to observe and provide feedback on the team's methods, processes, communications, and dynamics. Seek multiple perspectives and ideas from superiors, peers, subordinates, or others outside the organization to get a holistic view of a problem. Meet with team members to discuss alternate approaches to solving a problem or issue. Actively brainstorm ideas and encourage divergent thinking to develop creative solutions. Ask for performance feedback as a member of a planning or problem solving team.
Study	Observe a leader strong at implementing conceptual skills and models. Ask key questions about developing skill at conceptualizing problems and applying critical and creative thinking. Volunteer to be part of a project team addressing a complex issue requiring a creative solution. While working, observe the methods and processes used by the team and reflect on their effectiveness and possible improvements. Read references on how to expand conceptual and analytical skills, such as concept mapping, divergent thinking, systems thinking, or the military decisionmaking process. Access the Virtual Improvement Center to complete: Leadership Decision Making, The Value of Self-Awareness, or Beyond People Skills: Leveraging Your Understanding of Others.
Practice	Use reflective journaling as an aid for developing critical and creative thinking. Purposefully test new approaches and ideas for problem solving as the mission allows. Note which methods work best for different types of problems and circumstances. Incorporate lessons learned into processes. When providing guidance, identify known areas in need of improvement and have others determine how to avoid the same mistakes. Identify comprehensive, detailed solutions that account for multiple variables.

ANALYZES AND ORGANIZES INFORMATION TO CREATE KNOWLEDGE

7-54. Army leaders prepare themselves for leadership positions through life-long learning, which involves study and reflection in how best to acquire new knowledge (see table 7-37). Becoming a better learner involves several steps including planning a learning approach, focusing on specific and achievable learning goals, setting aside time to study, organizing new information as it is encountered, and tracking progress.

Table 7-37. Analyzes and organizes information to create knowledge

Strength Indicators	Need Indicators
Analyzes and synthesizes relevant source information, sees implications, and draws conclusions. Reflects on learning; organizes insights for future application. Identifies reliable sources of data and other resources to acquire knowledge. Implements strategies to learn new information faster and more thoroughly. Considers source, quality or relevance, and criticality of information to improve understanding.	Draws conclusions based on limited facts or an incomplete understanding of an issue. Organizes data for personal use rather than sharing resources. Does not document information sources. Ignores connections between pieces of information. Accepts information and assertions without critical review or thought to see if it makes sense.

Underlying Causes
Lacks a mental structure or frame of reference to organize, connect, and make sense of information. Assumes that sources are reliable without cross-referencing or checking them. Does not have the time to review newly learned information and organize it for future application. Applies past approaches and current knowledge rather than gain new knowledge and expanded perspectives. Does not understand how to determine or implement a plan or strategy for knowledge acquisition and sharing.

Feedback	Describe your understanding (such as facts, relationships, or mental models) of an important topic with a topical expert. Seek feedback on the completeness and accuracy of your understanding and advice on how to improve it further. Apply your understanding of a topic to predict emerging or anticipated events and their outcomes. Later compare predictions to actual outcomes and reflect on incorrect predictions: what information was misinterpreted or misapplied, what information was lacking, how to become better informed, and how to modify your mental models? Talk with experts in an area of interest who can provide recommendations on new resources or sources of knowledge relevant to the topic. Have them discuss how they used that information and translated it into practice.
Study	Read about methods of studying and reading to build understanding and insight. Investigate methods of categorizing and relating information to build mental models and systems understanding. Get instruction on how to conduct library and internet research to find relevant information Discuss, with an expert in an area of interest, methods, and criteria for evaluating the validity and usefulness of information. Access the Virtual Improvement Center to complete: Leadership Decision Making; The Value of Self-Awareness.
Practice	Develop a personal action plan that identifies personal information needs, how to obtain the information, and how you will study and synthesize it to produce needed knowledge and insights. Organize information and data as it is obtained. Do this by consciously looking for themes, principles, and connections. Make a concept map showing these elements and connections, then use this map as a way of organizing and making sense of newly acquired information. Develop a system for organizing, categorizing, integrating, and retrieving information that you need and use. This may involve filing, note taking, or databases. To organize and share information with others, consider online collaboration tools or interest groups. Use reviews to gather and make sense of important information from organizational events.

Maintains Relevant Cultural Awareness

7-55. In today's contemporary operational environment, it is critical for Army leaders to understand the culture in which they operate including awareness of partners, neutral parties, and adversaries. Army leaders must be mindful of cultural factors that may influence members of their unit, multinational partners, host nations and the local populace. Culturally astute leaders are able to more effectively utilize resources and complete the mission (see table 7-38).

Table 7-38. Maintains relevant cultural awareness

Strength Indicators	Need Indicators
Studies issues such as language, values, customs, ideas, beliefs, and patterns of thinking that influence self and others. Takes advantage of opportunities to expand knowledge of different cultures and languages. Stays current on cultural issues that contribute to successes or shortcomings in working with multinational partners and host nation citizens. Stays aware of current events, particularly those of international interest.	Fails to maintain an awareness of the effect culture factors can have on outcomes. Relies on tactical solutions without consideration of cultural influences. Views other cultures as inferior to own culture. Makes little or no attempt to learn about the cultures of adversaries and allies.

Underlying Causes
Underestimates, or fails to recognize, the influence that culture can play in shaping a person's values, behavior, ideas, beliefs, and patterns of thinking. Too busy to learn from previous encounters when cultural issues helped shape events. Personal way of thinking about culture and its influence on mission success is not aligned with Army doctrine. Believes that forces from partner nations will think and act like U.S. forces.

Feedback	Connect with an individual with whom you are comfortable from a different culture and discuss the social norms, mores, and expectations of their culture. Have the individual provide you with feedback on the degree of your cultural knowledge and sensitivity. Share what you have learned about other cultures with peers and subordinates. Encourage them to ask questions and provide insights related to your experiences. Take knowledge and skill tests as part of a formal language or culture-related course.
Study	Read about cultural awareness and the role that cross-cultural proficiency plays in influence and work across cultures, especially related to military operations. Read novels or short stories placed in and written by authors from cultures of interest. Join a club or professional association that fosters and encourages cross-cultural contact and understanding. Study a foreign language through a college, professional association, or computer-based learning opportunities. Seek information on the accompanying cultural norms and expectations. Take courses or engage in independent study of cultural anthropology, comparative religion, and other similar culture-spanning topics. Set aside a few hours each week dedicated to reading the news, paying particular attention to areas where America has national interests. Access the Virtual Improvement Center to complete: Seeking and Incorporating Diverse Ideas.
Practice	Consider subordinates' cultural backgrounds. Think about using a subordinate's particular background or experiences to increase the understanding and awareness of others and to accomplish the mission. Take advantage of cultural and language training courses and other learning opportunities. Discuss current cultural issues with subordinates and with other leaders. What effects do current issues have on unit effectiveness? What effect could they have in the future? Consider the historical evolution of other cultures and the functions that different elements of the culture serve in preserving the society. Make a personal inventory of your own opinions and create actionable steps to eliminate any obstacles you face that impede greater understanding of different people.

MAINTAINS RELEVANT GEOPOLITICAL AWARENESS

7-56. Today's military leaders are expected to operate in a variety of physical and cultural environments worldwide. To be prepared for worldwide deployment, military leaders must stay current on events and national policies around the world that may affect national interests or potentially lead to military intervention. This requires an understanding of American interests; an appreciation of international, political, and military processes; and study of relevant news from around the world (see table 7-39 on page 7-44).

Table 7-39. Maintains relevant geopolitical awareness

Strength Indicators	Need Indicators
Learns about societies, news, and events outside America through self-study. Can describe America's effects on other countries. Applies understanding of Army influences on other countries, multinational partners, and opposing forces in support of the mission. Understands factors that influence conflict and peacekeeping, peace enforcing, and peacemaking missions. Explains the implications and possible outcomes of geopolitical events to team members.	Demonstrates lack of awareness or concern for geopolitical issues and their relevance to military operations. Views military solutions as involving only the application of military power. Unaware of other American government agencies' contributions to planning and operations. Views countries as disconnected rather than mutually influencing components of a global system.

Underlying Causes
Unwilling or unskilled in using influence and negotiation to achieve mission objectives.   Embraces a limited and simplistic view of the scope of military objectives and methods.   Unaware of the influence and intricacies of the global political network.   Has trouble relating to other cultures or believes that personal culture is superior.   Views political issues, considerations, and behaviors as unsavory.

Feedback	Discuss geopolitical events with knowledgeable individuals to test personal perceptions and understanding of related facts and implications. When reviewing the effectiveness of mission performance or training events related to peacekeeping, peace enforcing, and peacemaking, examine the actual or likely political outcomes of decisions and unit's actions. Meet with the team to brainstorm creative solutions to any challenges the unit is facing or likely to face because of geopolitical events.
Study	Get in the habit of reading newspapers, news magazines, or online news sources. Make a point to seek out news on societal and political issues around the world. Research the cultures, physical resources, geography, histories, aspirations, policies, and geopolitical climates of the countries likely to affect national interests. Consider how other nations and cultures are reacting to current geopolitical events. How are other militaries acting or reacting? Access the Virtual Improvement Center to complete: Seeking and Incorporating Diverse Ideas
Practice	Lead group discussions on current geopolitical events. Consider questions such as: What driving factors are causing international conflicts? What cultures are involved? What role might the Army play in mitigating or resolving these conflicts? When making military decisions or planning military operations, consider how the methods and outcomes may affect American interests and international perceptions.

MAINTAINS SELF-AWARENESS

7-57. Self-aware leaders know themselves, including their traits, feelings, and behaviors. They employ self-understanding and recognize their effect on others. Self-aware leaders recognize their strengths and developmental needs across a range of environments and progressively use this knowledge to develop a clear, honest picture of capabilities and limitations (see table 7-40). Leaders must be flexible and adaptable by constantly assessing abilities and limitations in the context of mission requirements.

Table 7-40. Maintains self-awareness

Strength Indicators	Need Indicators
Actively evaluates one's strengths and developmental needs.	Unclear on personal and professional values, priorities, and objectives.
Learns from mistakes and makes corrections; learns from experience.	Is uncomfortable with the status quo; has no developmental direction or goals.
Considers feedback on performance, outcomes associated with actions, and actions taken by others to achieve similar goals.	Not attentive to the reaction of others.
	Completes tasks and moves on without reflecting on what went well and what could go better next time.
Determines personal goals and creates a path to achieve those goals.	Rejects or lacks interest in feedback.
Develops capabilities and seeks opportunities to improve in areas in need of development.	
Understands self-motivation under various conditions.	

Underlying Causes	
Fearful of identifying personal developmental needs or the effort required to resolve them.	
Does not think personal improvement is necessary.	
Disconnected or aloof from team members and subordinates.	
Not practiced or in the habit of self-observation, analysis, and reflection.	
Has personal blind spots or biases that block or distort self-observation, analysis, and reflection.	

Feedback	Seek feedback openly and actively by sitting down and informally talking with the team members and subordinates. Take a multi-source (360-degree) assessment, such as the Army's Multi-Source Assessment and Feedback instrument. Discuss one of your recent accomplishments or setbacks with a coach, friend, or other trusted individual who can provide you with honest feedback and encouragement. Analyze personal behaviors, performance, and interests to identify strengths and developmental needs. Share them with a trusted family member or associate and ask for their feedback.
Study	Keep an experience journal. Reflect on successful and unsuccessful situations. Write about events and describe what happened, how you reacted, how others reacted, and why. What can you learn about yourself based on what you did and how you felt? Self-analyze the gaps between your actual and desired self. Investigate ways that you can close those gaps using training, coaching, mentoring, books, and other learning materials. Analyze the actions of others in a variety of events. Think about the situations leading to the events, behaviors, and apparent motives during the events, and consequences or outcomes. Take time for personal reflection during your daily routine. Consider your recent thoughts and behaviors and how they relate to your values, priorities, and goals. Access the Virtual Improvement Center to complete: Seeking and Incorporating Diverse Ideas; Achieving Shared Understanding; The Art of Asking Questions; Building Working Relationships Across Boundaries; The Value of Self-Awareness; Seeking and Delivering Face-to-Face Feedback; Building Trust; Navigating Contentious Conversations; Beyond People Skills: Leveraging Your Understanding of Others.
Practice	Take a multi-source (360-degree) assessment, such as the Army's Multi-Source Assessment and Feedback instrument. Multi-source assessments collect data from peers, subordinates, superiors, and you to provide information on strengths and developmental needs. Create an individual development plan that identifies strengths and developmental needs and the activities to practice to achieve objectives. After important meetings or encounters, reflect on your statements and behaviors and their apparent effect on others. Reflect on your reactions to statements and behaviors. Find a coach to guide you through self-improvement. Good coaches know how to effectively collect and digest feedback and make it relevant and specific to you.

DEVELOPS OTHERS

7-58. Leaders encourage and support others to grow as individuals and teams. They facilitate the achievement of organizational goals through assisting others to develop. They prepare others to assume new positions elsewhere in the organization, making the organization more versatile and productive. This competency has four components:

- Assesses developmental needs of others.
- Counsels, coaches, and mentors.
- Facilitates ongoing development.
- Builds team skills and processes.

ASSESSES DEVELOPMENTAL NEEDS OF OTHERS

7-59. Regular counseling and evaluation of subordinates allows leaders to have a greater knowledge of their capabilities—including their strengths and limitations. This knowledge can help optimize Soldier and unit performance (via improved staffing decisions)—it demonstrates to Soldiers that leaders care about their performance and their development. Investing time and resources into team members' and subordinates' developmental needs fosters enhanced well-being for the individual and leads to improved unit and Army performance as a whole (see table 7-41).

Table 7-41. Assesses developmental needs of others

Strength Indicators	Need Indicators
Identifies subordinate internal drivers and uses those motivators to analyze developmental needs.	Gathers information about a subordinate's performance from only one source or only a few points in time.
Gathers information about a subordinate's development needs from multiple sources.	Assesses Soldiers on a small number of performance dimensions or competencies.
Reviews assessments or reports about a subordinate's interests or capabilities.	Reviews only one completed assessment or report.
Observes and monitors subordinates under different conditions.	Takes notice of subordinates only when challenged.
Helps subordinates develop individual development plans.	Generalizes subordinates' leadership patterns, strengths, and developmental needs based on limited observation.

Underlying Causes
Does not allocate the necessary time to get to know subordinates and understand their developmental needs.
Too busy to actively monitor subordinate performance on the full range of performance competencies.
Lacks a clear understanding of the subordinates' position requirements.
Uncomfortable delivering constructive feedback.
Time pressures hinder ability to provide immediate feedback.
Views an individual's continuous development as a low-ranking priority.

Feedback	Hold development discussions with subordinates at least once every three months. Integrate these discussions into the normal duty hours.
	Communicate to people that their work is important, even if it just means simply saying, "Thank you, I appreciate your hard work."
	Be open and tactfully forthright with people when discriminating between the developmental needs of subordinates. Make decisions in the best interest of the Army.
	Elicit input and feedback from subordinates on unit developmental needs.

Table 7-41. Assesses developmental needs of others (continued)

Study	Become familiar with personal and career goals of subordinates, as appropriate.
	Become knowledgeable of the roles, responsibilities, and requirements of subordinates' duties with which you are less familiar. This allows you to have a better understanding of what right looks like so you can better evaluate your Soldiers.
	During a usual workday, analyze the organization's overall approach to managing multiple priorities. How does this approach affect subordinates and their developmental needs?
	Observe another leader's behaviors during analysis of a subordinate's developmental needs. Analyze the communication skills used. Record the types of questions asked, language used, balance between positive and negative feedback, and time spent listening vice delivering feedback.
	Read a reference book or learn from listed resources.
	Access the Virtual Improvement Center to complete: Counseling and Coaching Videos.
Practice	Allocate time during the duty day to help subordinates create and implement an individual development plan. Be sure to have subordinates identify only one or two concrete goals at a time to build confidence and decrease frustration with vague, overly ambitious goals.
	Set up an office hour each week during which subordinates can freely come to talk with you about their developmental needs.
	Spend time each day among your Soldiers to observe their performance first-hand, talk with them about their duties, give immediate feedback, and talk with noncommissioned officers and junior officers in a good position to observe Soldier performance. This demonstrates to Soldiers that their performance is a priority.

COUNSELS, COACHES, AND MENTORS

7-60. Counseling, coaching, and mentoring stand as the principal ways by which leaders provide others with knowledge and feedback. Counseling occurs when leaders review with the subordinate their demonstrated performance and potential; coaching occurs when you guide another's development in new or existing skills during the practice of those skills; and mentoring occurs when you have greater experience than a mentee and guide and advise the mentee in their professional growth (see table 7-42).

Table 7-42. Counsels, coaches, and mentors

Strength Indicators	Need Indicators
Sets up regular counseling, coaching, or mentoring sessions with subordinates.	Inconsistently or infrequently sets up counseling sessions.
Clearly defines the purpose of a counseling, coaching, or mentoring session.	Counsels or mentors only those subordinates considered to have the most potential.
Encourages subordinates through actions while guiding them.	Uses a one-size-fits-all mentality when designing counseling, coaching, and mentoring sessions.
Helps an individual understand the current level of performance; Instructs and guides on how to reach the next level of knowledge and skill.	Fails to provide coaching and feedback during the workday—provides feedback only during scheduled sessions.
Candidly discusses a subordinate's strengths, developmental needs, and the courses of action to improve.	Avoids providing negative feedback.
	Talks at subordinates instead of with subordinates.
	Displays personal biases (such as likes, dislikes, or prejudices) and judges too rashly.

Underlying Causes
Busy with other duties (such as completing the mission) so that coaching, counseling, and mentoring have a lower priority.
Allocates insufficient time for counseling, coaching, and mentoring sessions.
Does not see value in spending time and resources on counseling, coaching, or mentoring subordinates perceived as having little potential.
Avoids personal conflict with subordinates; has difficulty telling subordinates things they may not want to hear.
Does not want to impose on subordinates' time with frequent follow-up calls or emails.

Table 7-42. Counsels, coaches, and mentors (continued)

Feedback	Ask peers about helpful training or learning materials they have experienced, whether it is civilian or military. Determine what they specifically found to be beneficial. Determine subordinates' attitudes toward counseling, coaching, and mentoring. If viewed negatively or as resources for the weak, set out a plan for changing that perception. Contact other units and find out how they have instituted and structured their counseling, coaching, or mentoring programs. Document this information and share it with the unit. Have a discussion with someone you have counseled, coached, or mentored in the past. Ask them to provide feedback on what you did right and what you could improve on.
Study	Identify individuals who served as counselors, coaches, and mentors to you. Document the actions they took to help you develop; identify those actions that were beneficial and analyze why that was the case. Study and read about counseling, coaching, or mentoring relationships in other, non-Army fields. Identify the qualities that counselors, coaches, and mentors in these fields exhibit and determine how you can best apply them. Next time you counsel, coach, or mentor a subordinate, take a moment following the session to record what you did and how the subordinate reacted. Reflect on your actions and the subordinate's responses to identify actions that could have used to improve the session. Actively observe how other leaders provide effective (or ineffective) coaching and feedback. Determine what could improve the effectiveness of the coaching or feedback. Access the Virtual Improvement Center to complete: Supporting the Developing Leader; Every Leader as a Coach; Counseling and Coaching Videos.
Practice	Schedule time to contact subordinates you counsel, coach, or mentor to regularly check-in and support their development. Consider sending an email as simple as "How's everything going? Let's catch up." Seek out on-duty or in-the-moment opportunities to reinforce or coach on specific issues, making links to broader developmental goals for that individual. Emphasize to subordinates the benefits of taking time to engage in developmental activities. Focus on the benefits it provides to both the unit and to the Army. Spend time walking around the unit each day. This provides opportunities to observe and providing immediate feedback and coaching to subordinates. Facilitate a unit culture that values feedback and coaching by evaluating subordinates (such as junior noncommissioned officers or officers) on the feedback and coaching they provide.

FACILITATES ONGOING DEVELOPMENT

7-61. As a learning institution, the Army seeks to continuously shape and develop their leaders to learn and adapt as conditions and operational environments evolve. Leaders must instill in subordinates a thirst for knowledge and continued development and must support them throughout the process (see table 7-43).

Table 7-43. Facilitates ongoing development

Strength Indicators	Need Indicators
Maintains awareness of existing individual and organizational development programs.	Fails to stay up-to-date on individual and organizational development programs.
Nominates and encourages subordinates to take advantage of developmental opportunities.	Displays ambivalence towards opportunities for self-development.
Arranges opportunities to help subordinates improve self-awareness, and competence.	Selects only some subordinates to take advantage of developmental opportunities.
Pushes tasks and decisions down to the lowest practical level to develop subordinates' capabilities and decisionmaking confidence.	Adopts an "I'll do it all" mentality—failing to identify tasks for delegation.
Identifies and removes obstacles to development.	Ignores obstacles to development.
Provides subordinates with (or directs them to) the necessary resources for development.	

Table 7-43. Facilitates ongoing development (continued)

	*Underlying Causes*

Underlying Causes
Unable to devote time to stay up-to-date on individual and organizational development programs.
Feels that the organization will suffer if too many members are engaged in developmental activities.
Feels that individual development should be left up to the individual.
Believes that mission or task effectiveness might suffer through delegation.
Is not personally affected by developmental obstacles so treats them as if they do not exist.

Feedback	Ask unit members to help identify any obstacles to development that exist. Request that they provide recommendations for eliminating the identified obstacles.
	Talk with subordinates you counsel, coach, or mentor. Ask what you can do to support their development and what you can do better to support unit development.
	Have a conversation with a superior about how well you are supporting development. Then ask them to share successful tips and tricks they have learned.
	Talk with a leader from another organization about ways to facilitate ongoing development. Share what you learned with your unit.
	Ask trusted unit members how supportive they think you and the organizational leadership are of training and development activities that occur during the workday and self-development that takes place on personal time.
Study	Allocate time to research development programs available to your subordinates. Recommend specific programs to individuals based on their developmental needs.
	Investigate the development practices of other organizations (such as sister Services or private sector companies) and incorporate their techniques if possible.
	Add leader development indicators to the unit training brief. Have subordinate units track and report on indicators of the health of leader development like other key unit systems (such as training, maintenance, and budget).
	Access the Virtual Improvement Center to complete: The Leader's Role in Providing On-the-Job Learning and Support; Supporting the Developing Leader; Creating and Supporting Challenging Job Assignments; Every Leader as a Coach; Enabling Subordinates Using Mission-Focused Delegation; Counseling and Coaching Videos.
Practice	Encourage subordinates of the same position to form a community-of-practice group and allocate training time to support them. Provide each group with an opportunity to present recommendations from their group to the leadership team.
	Encourage subordinates to hold others accountable for self-development, inquiring after development goals and actions and providing targeted feedback.
	Encourage other leaders and subordinates to use reflective journaling. Emphasize how it leads to greater self-awareness and serves as a reference for passing along lessons learned to others during times of transition or promotion.
	Hold brown bag lunches about various leadership and leader development topics. Solicit input from other leaders and subordinates regarding topics they would like to learn more about. Ask volunteers to present during the sessions.
	Have a subordinate help complete a task or make a decision to build confidence and competence.
	Encourage subordinates to support one another (as peers) during the implementation of their individual development plans.

BUILDS TEAM SKILLS AND PROCESSES

7-62. Building team skills and processes means that leaders inspire, motivate, and guide others toward accomplishing a common goal through cooperative efforts (see table 7-44). Effective cooperation and communication in (and between) teams facilitates unit success. Indeed, no single person, squad, platoon, company, battalion, or brigade ever won a war; it was the collaboration and teamwork at and between each level that enabled mission success.

Table 7-44. Builds team skills and processes

Strength Indicators	Need Indicators
Presents challenging assignments that require team interaction and cooperation.	Presents assignments that do not stretch the team beyond their comfort zones.
Sustains and improves the relationships among team members.	Provides minimal resources and support.
Facilitates effective and ongoing communication between team members.	Fails to spend sufficient time on group dynamics and relationships.
Provides realistic, mission-oriented training.	Focuses on the efforts and successes of individual subordinates.
Provides feedback on team processes.	Conducts training exercises, but never provides teamwork-specific feedback.
Emphasizes the importance of working together to achieve a "common purpose."	Fails to prioritize team goals over individual goals.

Underlying Causes
Does not have the time or desire to help teams accomplish challenging assignments.
More comfortable and experience teaching through lecture than through experiential activities.
Unaware of the importance of providing teamwork-specific feedback.
Feels that encouraging individual achievement is a more effective motivator than providing feedback and targeting motivation to groups or teams.
Does not communicate the importance of teamwork.

Feedback	Ask subordinates about activities they engage in outside of the Army that require teamwork. Then compile these examples, and share any best practices with the unit.
	Use an open-ended questionnaire to survey the unit and determine how well you are supporting team building and the improvement of group skills and processes. Use the answers to determine what is working well, what is not working, and how to enhance team performance.
	Following a training exercise, incorporate feedback specifically related to teamwork and skill building as part of the review.
	Whenever you conduct a training exercise, ensure that you reference the teamwork lessons learned when speaking with the unit. Reinforce lessons learned to ensure the unit remembers the role of teamwork in the activities they complete.
Study	Assess how well you interact with other leaders as part of a team. Although the command structure specifies the accountable individual in an Army team, are you soliciting input from lower-ranking team members and making them feel like their input is valued.
	Observe another leader engaging in a team-building exercise with their unit. Record the activities they perform and the feedback about what teams did well and what needs improvement.
	Study how teamwork and team building is used in other organizations or in other fields (such as sports teams or business organizations). Then document tips and strategies that stand out to you that could be adapted for unit use.
	Access the Virtual Improvement Center to complete: Rapid Team Stand-up: How to Build Your Team ASAP, Building Working Relationships across Boundaries, or Fostering Team Unity.
	ASAP: as soon as possible
Practice	Promote unit discussions about teamwork. Encourage subordinates to share their views on teams and the similarities and differences between teamwork and other types of collaboration (such as partnerships).
	Conduct frequent problem solving or brainstorming sessions with groups of subordinates (it is beneficial to change the composition of this group depending upon the problems or tasks discussed) to identify unit challenges and tasks, potential courses of action, strengths, developmental needs, and likely consequences associated with each.
	Emphasize to squads, platoons, or other teams in the unit that teamwork involves shared responsibility. There can be no blaming a bad team for not accomplishing a goal—each member of a team contributes to the success or failure.
	Dedicate time to develop Army-specific, realistic, and mission-oriented team building exercises for the unit.

STEWARDS THE PROFESSION

7-63. In planning, the Army requires its leaders to think beyond their current team, mission, and direct chain of leadership. Leaders steward the profession when they act to improve the organization even when the effects may not be realized until after their tenure. Stewarding the profession is about life-long learning, a commitment to an effective future organization, and developing others. This competency has two components:

- Supports professional and personal growth.
- Improves the organization.

SUPPORTS PROFESSIONAL AND PERSONAL GROWTH

7-64. Supporting institutional-based development means that leaders should focus on personal and subordinate development at both the macro- and micro-levels: leaders are responsible for the development of the Army as an institution (macro-level), and for the development of each individual (micro-level). By supporting the development, leaders strengthen the Army profession and ensure that it produces multi-skilled leaders, capable of adapting and excelling in a constantly changing strategic environment (see table 7-45).

Table 7-45. Supports professional and personal growth

Strength Indicators	Need Indicators
Encourages subordinates to pursue institutional learning opportunities and allows time to attend training. Provides information about institutional training and career progression to subordinates. Maintains resources related to institutional development. Participates in discussions across units to see the types of learning opportunities they recommend to their team members and subordinates. Updates team members and subordinates on learning opportunities that will occur.	Does not allow subordinates to attend institutional training or educational opportunities. Fails to stay up-to-date on individual and organizational development programs. Shows little personal interest in helping subordinates pursue institutional development opportunities. Tells subordinates to go find their own learning opportunities. Sends an implicit message to subordinates: self-development and organizational development are what Soldiers should focus upon; institutional training and education is a luxury.
Underlying Causes	
Providing Soldiers time to attend institutional training seems too large of a drain on the unit. Leader is too busy accomplishing the mission or task to be spending time thinking about the long-term developmental needs of subordinates. Belief that individual development is up to the individual and performed on personal time. Belief that subordinates should "learn by doing" rather than via institutional training.	
Feedback	Ask trusted subordinates to help identify obstacles to development. Request that they provide recommendations for eliminating the identified obstacles. Have a conversation with a superior about how well you are supporting development. Ask them to share tips and strategies that they have found to be effective. Talk with a leader from another unit about how to facilitate Soldier participation in professional military education without compromising unit effectiveness. Talk to subordinates about the benefits of institutional-based development: to meet and network with others outside their chain of command and share ideas and best practices.

Table 7-45. Supports professional and personal growth (continued)

Study	Think back to the last few times you nominated someone to take advantage of a developmental opportunity. Analyze your reasons for nominating them and the opportunities for which you nominated them. Look for patterns or potential biases. Ensure to set aside an appropriate amount of time to investigate available Army developmental opportunities so you are able talk about development with team members and subordinates. Remember that development does not equal training. Review opportunities for coaching, conference attendance, and scenario participation to provide a diverse set of activities. Solicit input from supervisors and peers on effectively managing Soldier attendance in institutional training and development while maintaining unit effectiveness. Access the Virtual Improvement Center to complete: The Leader's Role in Providing On-the-Job Learning and Support; Clarifying Roles; Supporting the Developing Leader; Every Leader as a Coach; Counseling and Coaching Videos.
Practice	Identify key leadership positions in the command to conduct and manage succession planning. Chart the timing and sequencing of subordinates into and out of leadership positions and schedule subordinates in institutional training programs accordingly. Maintain an institutional development resource binder of resources offered by the Army related to development. This could include counseling, coaching, or mentoring programs or opportunities or training courses offered. Send out periodic reminders to subordinates to enroll in selected training opportunities. Create a calendar of Army-based training opportunities and post it in a central location. Champion learning by encouraging others to attend training opportunities.

IMPROVES THE ORGANIZATION

7-65. Leaders demonstrate stewardship when they act to improve the organization for not only the present but also the future Army (see table 7-46). Acting to improve the organization involves prioritizing and managing people and resources when the effect may not be immediately evident. Leaders who steward the profession have a lasting concern over how their decisions affect the organization's future.

Table 7-46. Improves the organization

Strength Indicators	*Need Indicators*
Demonstrates commitment to the organization and others by attitude, beliefs, and behaviors. Is future thinking, articulates a future for the organization. Possesses the leadership characteristics of self-sacrifice and vision. Prioritizes the future of the organization beyond immediate, personal goals. Considers the effects of decisions carefully.	Fails to take time to develop others. Takes an apathetic posture to the future of the unit and the Army. Fails to articulate a vision for the future. Appears overly self-focused. Does not seem concerned about unit morale. Fails to be conscientious in decisionmaking.

Underlying Causes	
Overly focused on self and personal ambitions. Fear of the unknown, an unwillingness to shape the future. Lack of vision; narrow focus. Impulsive. Impatient to cultivate slow-growing positive effects.	

Feedback	Seek informal feedback constantly from subordinates on the effects of decisions. Understand how personal decisions reverberate down the chain of command. Seek counsel from mentors and trusted peers. Ask them what they do to ensure the future unit success beyond their tenure. Describe your own actions and get feedback. Hold informal, periodic meetings with subordinates to discuss unit vision. Get feedback on current policies and practices to implement that vision, and possible obstacles.

Table 7-46. Improves the organization (continued)

Study	Study the actions of leaders you admire. Note their approaches to improve the organization (such as support growth through leader development). Consider applying a similar approach.
	Study the nature of the unit in its present state. Consider the major differences between the present and envisioned unit. Improving the organization is about narrowing that gap.
	Study Army policy and guidance. Prepare for the future by measuring the gap between the current unit status and future requirements. Then, determine what actions to take.
	Access the Virtual Improvement Center to complete: Clarifying Roles, Creating and Promulgating a Vision of the Future, Building Working Relationships across Boundaries.
Practice	Have a vision for the future of the unit. Regularly communicate that future in staff meetings and via other outlets such as newsletters and emails.
	Make decisions beneficial to the unit, particularly where the rewards might not immediately available within your tenure as leader.
	Invest in people. Support personal and professional growth linked to improving the organization.

GETS RESULTS

7-66. A leader's ultimate purpose is to get results by accomplishing missions the right way. A leader gets results by providing guidance and managing resources as well as demonstrating the other leader competencies. This competency focuses on consistent and ethical task accomplishment through supervising, managing, monitoring, and guiding the team's work. Taken together, these components require initiative on the part of the leader to make decisions, take action to solve problems, and accomplish the mission:

- Prioritizes, organizes, and coordinates taskings for teams or other organizational groups.
- Identifies and accounts for individual and group capabilities and commitment to task.
- Designates, clarifies, and deconflicts duties and responsibilities.
- Identifies, contends for, allocates, and manages resources.
- Removes work obstacles.
- Recognizes and rewards good performance.
- Seeks, recognizes, and takes advantage of opportunities to improve performance.
- Makes feedback part of work processes.
- Executes plans to accomplish the mission.
- Identifies and adjusts to external influences on the mission and organization.

PRIORITIZES, ORGANIZES, AND COORDINATES TASKINGS

7-67. Leaders are responsible for coordinating all of the simultaneous undertakings of their team and resourcing subordinates to complete the mission properly. Army leaders must be detailed planners who actively organize and communicate priorities to their team to ensure task execution in the right place, at the right time, in the right operational environment (see table 7-47 on page 7-54).

Table 7-47. Prioritizes, organizes, and coordinates taskings

Strength Indicators	Need Indicators
Breaks down work into process steps or tasks. Accurately scopes out length, sequence, and difficulty of tasks to achieve desired outcomes. Sets goals and clear objectives that are specific, measurable, and time bound. Develops schedules, assigns tasks, and organizes individuals to accomplish tasks. Facilitates subordinate and team task accomplishment without over-specification and micromanagement.	Operates "in the moment" without deliberate thought of how to complete the task. Fails to identify road blocks that delay or prevent task accomplishment. Does not develop a plan of action when coordinating tasks across teams and groups. Reassigns tasks to different teams without evaluating the effect on existing workload and priorities. Closely and excessively controls the work of subordinate staff.

Underlying Causes
Functions as a part of the reactionary environment; does not seek to be proactive. Does not hold a clear sense of desired outcomes. Procrastinates; manages time ineffectively. Operates in isolation; does not effectively delegate. Does not take time to see how all of the moving pieces fit together as a whole.

Feedback	Ask trusted peers or superiors for an assessment of your judgment and planning skills. Request a recommendation on ways to improve. Get a backbrief from subordinates after issuing directions, warning orders, or operations orders. Seek feedback on how you influence others in a way that promotes accomplishment of the organization's purpose or mission. Ask others how effective you are at providing purpose, direction, and motivation to team members. While planning and coordinating, continually ask yourself, "Who else needs to (or should) know about this?" Keep them informed. After completing a series of tasks, request feedback from individuals and groups on what went well and what to improve.
Study	Review the steps of the military decisionmaking process to plan for an upcoming project or task. Reflect on the mission, goals, and commander's vision for the organization and the next higher organization. How do they influence prioritization of tasks? Assess the skills, talents, capabilities, values, personalities, motivations, and needs of team members. Use this information to make decisions about task assignments, responsibilities, and how much latitude or supervision to give. Observe leaders who manage multiple tasks effectively. Discuss the practices they use to ensure success. Incorporate these practices to manage multiple tasks and priorities. Access the Virtual Improvement Center to complete: Accounting for Differences in Capabilities and Commitment, The Leader's Role in Providing On-the-Job Learning and Support; Removing Work Barriers; Rapid Team Stand-up: How to Build Your Team ASAP; Fostering Team Unity, Enabling Subordinates Using Mission-Focused Delegation; Out of Time: Managing Competing Demands. ASAP: as soon as possible
Practice	When starting a new task, define responsibilities and expectations by providing clear guidance on what to accomplish, the parameters for getting it done, and expectations for the outcome. Then ask for feedback and concerns about task accomplishment. Ensure understanding by asking for a backbrief from key members. When faced with multiple tasks, develop a project plan that details how to execute tasks. Consider resources available (including time), the level of personnel support, and potential obstacles. Before starting, convey task priority to the team. Develop the sequence of the tasks that are dependent upon one another. List tasks in the order of an optimal progression to prioritize what to accomplish first. Set up a process to monitor progress on a task or project against a project plan. Anticipate the potential problems that may arise during the execution of a task. During the planning phase, determine ways to prevent the problems from occurring or how to resolve them effectively and efficiently should they occur.

IDENTIFIES AND ACCOUNTS FOR INDIVIDUAL AND GROUP CAPABILITIES AND COMMITMENT TO TASK

7-68. Matching individuals and groups to a task can be a challenging undertaking, particularly when it comes to analyzing the capabilities of a unit or organization. Having a clear understanding of the task is important to identify both individual and group capabilities and developmental needs. It is important for leaders to understand a team's individual interests to use their knowledge, skills, and abilities effectively as well as work towards their developmental needs (see table 7-48).

Table 7-48. Identifies and accounts for capabilities and commitment to task

Strength Indicators	Need Indicators
Considers duty positions, capabilities, and developmental needs when assigning tasks. Assesses skills, capabilities, and developmental needs when beginning a new task or assuming a new position. Assigns individuals or groups to tasks so that their skills match the task or project requirements.	Assigns tasks without accounting for individuals' interests and abilities. Resources projects without getting a clear commitment that tasks will finish when required. Delegates under the assumption that all staff hold the same level of capability and commitment. Does not match project needs with individual interests and developmental needs. Assumes that subordinate lack of commitment to a task means they are disinterested.

Underlying Causes	
Assumes all individuals possess similar levels of capability and commitment. Too busy to stay apprised of personnel capabilities and commitment levels. Too busy to assess subordinates' duty and role requirements when assuming a new leadership position. Is unaware of both individual and group interests and developmental needs. Does not see the benefit in following up with staff on their progress toward completing a task.	

Feedback	Talk with others who may know your subordinates and have them provide insight about their skills and interests. Check their perceptions against your own assessment. Ask peers and subordinates about their commitment to performing a task. Do not assume their level of commitment or interest. Objectively observe your own behavior managing workloads and leading subordinates. Do you match individuals with tasks and projects that interest them and match their capabilities? Get feedback to compare with your self-assessment.
Study	Develop knowledge and expertise regarding the duty and role requirements of subordinate positions. Document the degree to which current capabilities match requirements. Observe subordinates at work. Evaluate their capabilities and motivations. Assess the skills, talents, capabilities, motivations, and needs of members of the team. Use this information to make decisions about task assignments, responsibilities, and how much latitude or supervision to give. Evaluate the skill sets needed to complete a project and match the skills with the capabilities and level of commitment of team members available to work on the project. Access the Virtual Improvement Center to complete: The Leader's Role in Providing On-the-Job Learning and Support; Accounting for Differences in Capabilities and Commitment; Creating and Supporting Challenging Job Assignments; Rapid Team Stand-up: How to Build Your Team ASAP; Enabling Subordinates Using Mission-Focused Delegation. ASAP: as soon as possible
Practice	The next time routine task requirements occur, rotate subordinates through different roles to identify their skills, capabilities, and developmental needs. Pair up individuals with greater and lesser skills so team members will have the benefit of teaching and learning from each other. Match individuals to tasks or projects by assigning team members with complementary skills to work together to ensure all skill requirements are met. Reallocate resources on a task or assignment to ensure that people do not become complacent. Make work assignments to train team members to be multifunctional.

DESIGNATES, CLARIFIES, AND DECONFLICTS DUTIES AND RESPONSIBILITIES

7-69. Designating, clarifying, and deconflicting duties and responsibilities is an important leadership behavior because it improves a team's satisfaction and performance by removing ambiguity and confusion related to who is supposed to do what, at what time, and in what location (see table 7-49). Designating, clarifying, and deconflicting duties and responsibilities also improves a team's motivation and commitment as it ensures that team members know they are expected to contribute to the mission.

Table 7-49. Designates, clarifies, and deconflicts duties and responsibilities

Strength Indicators	Need Indicators
Explains how subordinate roles support the unit's goals and work of others.	Provides subordinates with competing demands or contradictory messages about their role.
Establishes procedures for monitoring, coordinating, and regulating subordinates' activities.	Maintains a sink or swim attitude.
Informs subordinates of work expectations, particularly when taking on a new role.	Does not define or clearly communicate roles, desired outcomes, and goals to team members.
Successfully resolves subordinate conflicts regarding duty tasks or roles.	Assigns tasks without determining if work is in the scope of an individual's abilities.
Clearly outlines responsibilities and desired outcomes.	Refuses to be involved in subordinate conflicts and disagreements about "who does what."

Underlying Causes
Does not conceptualize how contributions of team members should fit together.
Unable to see the benefit of providing a clear message or guidance on role expectations.
Over-tasked (or under-tasked) and not able to allocate distinct work roles.
Lacks knowledge of position requirements and personnel capabilities when assigning work.
Uninterested in managing work or people.

Feedback	Assess workload across teams and individuals. Do some have too much or too little?
	Ask subordinates if they are experiencing role conflict. Attempt to identify the causes.
	Capitalize on existing group communication mechanisms such as staff meetings, weekly status reports, and informal check-ins. Use these opportunities to assess and gain feedback on role clarity and shared understanding of responsibilities.
	After defining roles and duties for a new operation or process, ask for feedback on how well the roles are defined and distinctive before making assignments.
Study	Analyze the working relationships, processes, and outcomes of individuals and teams to identify potential role conflict or stress.
	Consider subordinates and their work processes. Are role expectations in line with their abilities?
	Evaluate a current performance problem with an individual or team and consider whether the problem relates to unclear or overlapping roles and responsibilities.
	Examine the goals and desired end states the team is currently pursuing. Are current work assignments appropriate given the requirements of the broader mission?
	Study the workload shouldered by team members. Is there a balance in the duties and tasks? Do some individuals have roles that are responsible for too much work or not enough work?
	Access the Virtual Improvement Center to complete: Removing Work Barriers, Clarifying Roles, Managing Conflict, Rapid Team Stand-up: How to Build Your Team ASAP, or Building Working Relationships across Boundaries.
	ASAP: as soon as possible
Practice	When assigning tasks or projects, make a list of those who will contribute to each defined objective and what specifically they will do to complete the team's task.
	Meet with subordinates who are unclear on their role or expected duties. Discuss and clarify their role, the difference from other roles, and the collective contribution to the desired outcome.
	When placing a subordinate in a new role or increasing their level of responsibility, proactively identify role requirements. Help the subordinate create a plan to fulfill expectations.
	When tasks transfer from one person or team to another, clarify or redefine the objectives.
	Ask subordinates or team members to list the duties and responsibilities associated with their current roles. Review the lists and confirm the accuracy to each subordinate. As needed, redefine or clarify the expectations of each role.

IDENTIFIES, CONTENDS FOR, ALLOCATES, AND MANAGES RESOURCES

7-70. One of a leader's main responsibilities is to accomplish the mission using the available resources in the most effective and efficient way possible (see table 7-50). Some Army leaders specialize in managing single categories of resources, such as ammunition, food, or finances, but everyone has an interest in seeing teams use all categories of resources wisely. A leader's resources include labor, money, and time.

Table 7-50. Identifies, contends for, allocates, and manages resources

Strength Indicators	Need Indicators
Allocates adequate time, money, and personnel for task completion.	Wastes time, money, material, and individual productivity.
Keeps track of people, equipment, material, and other resources.	Inconsistently allocates resources; plays favorites.
Gets things done with less; figures out effective and efficient ways to accomplish work.	Allocates resources without understanding or evaluating what and when resources are needed.
Allocates resources objectively by evaluating priorities and needs presented by the situation.	Does not track resource usage nor communicate status to superiors, subordinates, or others who have a need or interest to know.
Negotiates when it is necessary to allocate resources.	Hesitates to make important resource decisions.

Underlying Causes
Relies heavily on managing a single specialty, such as personnel or finance, but does not have a comprehensive understanding of other resources.
Is disorganized and does not have or use good resource tracking systems.
Feels pressured or obligated to allocate resources to a certain priority.
Does not know how to create alignment among objectives, activities, and outcomes.
Is slow in making decisions, even with adequate facts and information.

Feedback	After task completion, get input on how resources were used. Did the resources advance the mission? Were the resources squandered or used effectively? Communicate openly with superiors, subordinates or others by holding periodic updates to discuss project status. Include agenda bullets such as budget tracking, personnel constraints, and timeline risks. Discuss project or task milestones with team members. Determine if they have the necessary resources to deliver on their work. Hold a review to analyze how the team managed resources on a recent project or task. Identify strengths and areas for improvement for next time.
Study	Study how other units and organizations plan and allocate resources. Decide how you could apply other approaches to your work. Examine how you handle situations and reactions from individuals who may feel their requests for resources were not handled fairly or effectively. Develop key points on your reasons for allocating resources and prepare to discuss them with individuals. Identify project milestones and evaluate the status of resources against the milestone and baseline. If resources are not on target, evaluate if they need reallocation. Study resource allocations (personnel, cost, time, money, and materials) you will need in the planning phase of a mission or tasking. Identify who controls the resources. Study how you and others spend time. What types of tasks are the biggest time wasters? Are any of lesser importance or criticality, and do they adversely affect the task? Determine how to use time more efficiently. Access the Virtual Improvement Center to complete: Rapid Team Stand-up: How to Build Your Team ASAP, Leadership Decision Making, or Out of Time: Managing Competing Demands. ASAP: as soon as possible
Practice	Identify the individuals who will contribute to a project and what they will do. Next, identify required resources (such as time, equipment, or training) to complete the project and how these resources will best be allocated. Reallocate resources on a task or assignment to balance workload across the team with the goal of developing team members into multifunctional operators. Practice resource leveling when allocating resources to ensure a steady level of staffing, resource spending, and no crunched deadlines.

REMOVES WORK OBSTACLES

7-71. A work obstacle is anything that stands in the way of getting the task done (see table 7-51). Army leaders must remove or find ways to overcome a variety of obstacles including resource shortages; competing or conflicting tasks; personnel issues; new requirements, regulations, or policies; lack of integration among different branches of an organization; and a failure to synchronize and coordinate efforts.

Table 7-51. Removes work obstacles

Strength Indicators	Need Indicators
Declines tasking requests that would overburden the unit or distract it from its primary mission.	Accepts tasking requests from superiors that distract or overburden the unit or organization.
Is proactive in recognizing and resolving scheduling conflicts and resource and personnel challenges.	Leaves subordinates to figure out ways to deal with completing or conflicting tasks.
Asks for input on effective solutions to overcome work obstacles.	Does not recognize or address work obstacles when they first appear.
Checks in with trusted subordinates to ensure they are not overburdened.	Does not maintain close contact with trusted subordinates; loses touch with unit.

Underlying Causes
Wants to please, impress, and create a positive impression to superiors; is afraid to say no to requests.
Lacks focus. Works on issues as they come up.
Is a procrastinator. Puts off addressing a work obstacle until it becomes a crisis.
Sees problem situations as insurmountable, not as challenges that to overcome.
Is resistant to handle or deal with a work obstacle particularly discussing it with leaders at a higher level.
Has a short-term view. Does not see how current problems or obstacles affect long-term results.

Feedback	After identifying a work obstacle, talk to subordinates and find out more details about how the obstacle affects their role and their ability to complete the mission.
	Identify a work obstacle affecting the group. Meet with a superior or peers to discuss potential solutions. Ask for feedback on the how likely each solution is to be successful.
	Brainstorm creative ways to mitigate, buffer, and reduce the effect of the obstacle with the team. Have subordinates provide their own ideas and feedback.
	Get feedback on the original project or work plan. When encountering an obstacle determine required resources and processes to obtain them.
	Get input on your personal effectiveness in removing or reducing an obstacle. What worked well? What could you have done to be more effective?
Study	Document a potential ripple effect of new requirements or taskings on the unit to see if the mission, work, or goals are still achievable.
	Identify who will be affected by a new requirement or work obstacle. Document how each entity could be affected and possible solutions to minimize unintended outcomes.
	Conduct a broader analysis of a work obstacle to understand who (such as other units or stakeholders) could be affected. Identify individuals or groups from whom you could request support and what they could provide.
	Access the Virtual Improvement Center to complete: Removing Work Barriers; Out of Time: Managing Competing Demands.
Practice	Set up a process to monitor progress against plans. Search for new and innovative ways to help reduce, avoid, and overcome obstacles.
	Prioritize tasks based on their importance or relation to the mission. Be willing to accept deferring some lower priority tasks to a later date.
	Be open to suggestions that offer alternative actions and solutions to address a work obstacle.
	Actively seek the counsel of senior subordinates to identify current and potential obstacles and ways to overcome (or remove) them.

RECOGNIZES AND REWARDS GOOD PERFORMANCE

7-72. Leaders usually regard rewards as incentives to influence the behavior of others so they will perform in ways that are desirable and beneficial to the organization (see table 7-52). They serve as a benefit to Army leaders and team members who work to achieve more than is normally expected. Often, rewards relate closely to motivation and morale and can make an organization a place where its members strive to achieve results.

Table 7-52. Recognizes and rewards good performance

Strength Indicators	Need Indicators
Deflects credit or praise to those subordinates most responsible for unit successes.	Takes credit for unit or team accomplishments and successes.
Recognizes individual and team accomplishment and provides rewards appropriately.	Creates and promulgates an environment that accepts favoritism.
Gives clear, specific performance feedback so staff understand why they are recognized.	Recognizes only failures or poor performance.
Takes into account others' motivations and recognition preferences.	Rewards only individuals and does not recognize team accomplishments.
Knows the Army's performance systems and explores other reward systems.	Does not see a relationship between positive recognition, motivation, and morale.
Looks for ways to build on team and individual successes.	

Underlying Causes	
Is unaware of the value of recognition and reward for good work as part of leadership. Unable to see the link between reward and recognition and increased performance or productivity. Pays little attention to monitoring or observing subordinates. Does not treat people as individuals or recognize that different types of rewards and recognition motivate different individuals.	

Feedback	Get feedback from subordinates on their grasp of the performance standards for their work. Recognize that rewards are specific to each individual, so it is important to understand what specific motivators are particularly "rewarding" for each individual. Self-assess your approach to rewarding and recognizing subordinates. Observe factors like how often success is recognized, who is recognized, and the types of rewards used. Acknowledge what individuals or teams contribute; relate appropriate rewards. Before recognizing an individual or team, discuss your justification and rationale for the reward with a trusted leader who is familiar with the situation. Ask for feedback on your justification and rationale. Ask subordinates to share their reaction upon receiving a reward. Did they understand and agree with the performance standards and rationale for the reward? Did they think the reward was appropriate given the accomplishment?
Study	Observe subordinates to determine what motivates them. Since subordinates are motivated by different things, document what you believe motivates each member. Consider how to reward individuals and teams. Reward desired behaviors. For example, organizations often stress the importance of teamwork but reward exemplary individuals rather than teams. Create a matrix that matches members of the team and the reward types they value most. Analyze whether an accomplishment was due to one or several individuals or a team. Identify a unit member that appears to successfully reward and recognize superior performance. How does their behavior compare to yours in providing rewards and recognition? Access the Virtual Improvement Center to complete: Motivating through Rewards.
Practice	Reward high achievement rather than routine work. Devise appropriate rewards for both individuals and teams. Create rewards or incentives that boost subordinate morale and motivation. Consider granting time off, recognizing birthdays, and planning team events. Regularly walk around work areas to observe productivity, provide feedback, and praise when appropriate. Provide on-the-spot praise or awards for work that exceeds expectations. Reward instances where subordinates demonstrate innovative thought or creativity in their approach, even if unsuccessful. This conveys to others that these attributes are valued.

SEEKS, RECOGNIZES, AND TAKES ADVANTAGE OF OPPORTUNITIES TO IMPROVE PERFORMANCE

7-73. The individual who recognizes and takes advantage of opportunities to improve performance is a strong critical thinker who recognizes each completed task as a learning experience to improve upon in the future. Army leaders must simultaneously be proactive and reflective to seize and take advantage of opportunities when they occur (see table 7-53).

Table 7-53. Seeks, recognizes, and takes advantage of opportunities

Strength Indicators	Need Indicators
Employs skills and approaches fitting the situation. Gains support from individuals outside the unit when new or different skills are needed. Is open to others' ideas and sees how new ideas can improve the unit's performance. Knows strengths and limitations; uses strengths to improve performance. Reviews what worked well and what to improve.	Never asks others how processes, conditions, or situations could be improved. Manages without seeing the bigger picture, relationships among activities, and alignment of objectives and activities with outcomes. Tries to complete too many tasks at once; does not budget time for planning and reflection.

Underlying Causes
Uncomfortable taking risks; does not like to propose alternative solutions for fear of failure. Prefers the current routine or status quo, hesitant to implement change. Does not identify and track the current and future states of projects and tasks. Is too busy to devote time to consider or implement ways to improve performance. Is unaware of the opportunities to improve performance that exist.

Feedback	After completion of a particular project or task, hold an after action review. Specifically identify and discuss ways to improve performance the next time. Discuss opportunities to improve performance with team members. Have members identify a problem they think affects performance. Get feedback before recommending improvements. Self-assess the recent contributions of the team toward the organization's mission. Ask, "What small change would make the greatest difference? What time is available to make a change? What types of changes can I affect? What will I commit to?" Discuss with others what you can do to improve performance. Learn about actions taken by others that worked and others that did not work. If an individual has a performance problem. meet with them to identify the reasons behind the problem. Get feedback on specific steps they will take to correct the problem and improve.
Study	Create a project plan documenting what needs to happen throughout the project lifecycle to anticipate needed actions and how to achieve the desired outcome. Research the best method for developing strategies to achieve tasks. Discuss possible solutions with peers and senior subordinates. Write an improvement plan for the organization and outline how to improve certain internal practices. Evaluate the plan with input from others. Analyze the ideal state of the organization. What should success look like? Develop a visual map for a process. Are steps sequenced appropriately? Are intermediate steps needed? Look for loopholes or obstacles in the process. Access the Virtual Improvement Center to complete: Fostering Team Unity.
Practice	Use communication tools to share available information with group members on opportunities to improve performance. Provide subordinates with regular and consistent feedback on their strengths, where they meet the standard, and their developmental needs. Try a new approach to improve the performance of others, and see how it works. Adjust the approach, as needed, after getting feedback. Remember there are no bad ideas. Ask comprehensive questions to gauge how realistic an idea is and how easy or difficult it will be to implement. Conduct periodic brainstorming sessions with subordinates to identify common or recurring problems and likely causes. Encourage creative ideas and solutions.

MAKES FEEDBACK PART OF WORK PROCESSES

7-74. Consistent and regular feedback provided through coaching, counseling and mentoring has multiple benefits (see table 7-54). First, feedback helps a person improve at their position by identifying specific areas in which they excel as well as those in need of improvement. Feedback also helps to gauge subordinate engagement, motivation, and morale. The exchange of feedback keeps leaders informed on an organization's collective strengths and developmental needs.

Table 7-54. Makes feedback part of work processes

Strength Indicators	Need Indicators
Gives and seeks accurate and timely feedback.	Comments on subordinates' personal characteristics and not their work behaviors.
Uses feedback to modify duties, tasks, and procedures where appropriate.	Provides feedback infrequently or only during official performance reviews.
Provides regular, ongoing feedback and coaching to subordinates to increase their awareness of performance.	Tends to provide only positive or only negative feedback.
Uses assessment techniques and evaluation tools, such as after action reviews, to identify lessons learned and facilitate continuous improvement.	Does not provide the subordinate with clear feedback on what success looks like.
	Provides feedback without considering an appropriate setting or time.
	Ignores reviews and other evaluation tools (is not incorporated into modifications of procedures).

Underlying Causes
Overworked and unable to find the time to give feedback.
Unaware of the relationships between frequent and consistent feedback, subordinate motivation and morale, and improving performance.
Feels uncomfortable providing negative feedback or discussing areas for improvement.
Believes feedback should be corrective (such as what is not working) rather than supportive.
Lacks knowledge in how to deliver constructive feedback to guide subordinates toward success.

Feedback	Get feedback from subordinates on the frequency and quality of the performance feedback you provide. Determine if subordinates consider your feedback helpful and timely. Are they using it to modify their behaviors?
	Informally gain input from the team after completing a task or project. Collect the input first without offering feedback. Use information in a formal after action review.
	Self-assess the frequency and quality of feedback you provide. Notice how often you give feedback, to whom and when, and indications of how it was received. Seek counsel of a trusted senior subordinate to verify and validate your self-assessment.
	Ensure that your subordinates understand what you communicate by using a feedback loop or asking a question such as "How will you implement this? What will you take away from our discussion? What changes do you plan to make immediately?"
	Observe the actions of someone who provides accurate, effective, and frequent feedback. Watch their actions and feedback methods. Determine if there are aspects of their approach that you may be able to adopt and incorporate.
	Observe subordinates' work to determine their strengths and developmental needs. Document and prioritize needs. Identify candidates for immediate feedback and coaching.
Study	Study the principles and techniques of active listening.
	Study subordinates' behaviors when giving feedback. What nonverbal behaviors do they demonstrate? Determine if they demonstrate openness or reluctance to accept feedback. Consider how to adjust feedback to ensure receipt of the message.
	Take a course with situational exercises and role-plays that have participants practice delivering feedback. Learn to give feedback effectively by doing.
	Access the Virtual Improvement Center to complete: The Leader's Role in Providing On-the-Job Learning and Support; Supporting the Developing Leader; Seeking and Delivering Face-to-Face Feedback.

Table 7-54. Makes feedback part of work processes (continued)

Practice	Use the seven pillars of effective feedback. Be constructive, objective, specific, timely, considerate, future-oriented, and make sure that feedback is ongoing.
	Create a schedule outlining key project milestones. Provide feedback to the team members and subordinates shortly following each milestone.
	Provide feedback that will improve tomorrow's performance, not fix yesterday's. Ensure feedback enables subordinates to determine their next steps for development.
	Practice giving praise for positive performance. Describe specific positive behaviors, their results, and the effect on work products or team efforts.
	Identify unique situations, such as a typically high performing subordinate who is struggling with one aspect of their position and tailor feedback accordingly. Provide feedback and actively listen to the subordinate describe the situation.

EXECUTES PLANS TO ACCOMPLISH THE MISSION

7-75. Proper execution of plans to accomplish the mission involves careful task management to ensure plans are implemented effectively and efficiently through the task lifecycle. This involves managing the scope, schedule, time, cost, quality, risk, communications, human resources, and project integration. Army leaders must be organized and clear in their requests of others, ensuring that all issues are handled proactively and that the project is carefully monitored to ensure alignment with the desired outcomes (see table 7-55).

Table 7-55. Executes plans to accomplish the mission

Strength Indicators	Need Indicators
Schedules activities to meet all commitments in critical performance areas.	Over-reliance on personal contributions to execute plans; ineffectively involves others.
Notifies team members in advance when their support is required.	Unaware of how various activities come together.
Keeps track of task assignments and suspenses.	Provides plans too late for others to provide support.
Adjusts assignments, if necessary.	Rushes at the last minute to complete work and activities to achieve an objective; constantly putting out fires.
Evaluates work progress and accomplishments against plans.	Disorganized and unable to see factors that affect plans.
Attends to details that affect the plan.	

Underlying Causes
Lacks experience to track the current and future state of a project or tasking.
Is unable or unwilling to plan for second and third order effects.
Does not bring the multiple activities together at the right time to achieve objectives.
Lacks ability to be creative and resourceful when problems arise.
Does not use basic project management tools actively or consistently.
Does not effectively delegate or seek assistance before a crisis develops.

Feedback	Ask trusted peers or superiors for their assessment of your judgment and planning skills and discuss ways to improve.
	After subordinates work on a task, get feedback on their progress through observation, asking them directly, or asking others. Adjust roles or assignments as needed.
	Monitor progress against objectives, progress against milestones, resource use and costs, and human performance by compiling monthly reports that document each area.
	Seek feedback from superiors, peers, and subordinates on how well you notify them when your projects are on target for completion or in need of support.

Table 7-55. Executes plans to accomplish the mission (continued)

Study	Observe other leaders who effectively develop project plans and handle multiple tasks efficiently. What aspects of their approach work well? What can you do to adapt their approach?
	Review all projects, missions, and objectives to ensure they have measurable, specific, achievable outcomes. Identify required resources (such as time, personnel, or equipment) to achieve the desired outcome.
	Evaluate your ability to be flexible when unplanned events and problems develop. Decide how ready you are to change direction or tactics.
	Study historical figures that successfully achieved high profile victories. Read about large-scale failures. What made these leaders successful or unsuccessful in accomplishing the mission? What factors led to effective or ineffective planning and follow-through?
	Research various project management tools and software to find resources that help you to plan for and execute missions.
	Access the Virtual Improvement Center to complete: Leadership Decision Making, Being an Adaptable Leader in Times of Change, Out of Time: Managing Competing Demands.
Practice	Use a tracking system or tools to monitor activities and schedules and timetables.
	Be aware and recognize potential conflicts in the project plan before a problem occurs. Take preventive action when you foresee complications to the project plan.
	Manage time more effectively using a calendar, spreadsheet, or Gantt chart.
	Share successful outcomes with others involved throughout the completion of a task.

IDENTIFIES AND ADJUSTS TO EXTERNAL INFLUENCES ON THE MISSION OR TASKINGS AND ORGANIZATION

7-76. Being able to identify and adjust to external influences on the mission or taskings and organization requires a certain degree of flexibility and adaptability (see table 7-56). Using a logical and methodical mental process to document the changing environment is useful in making necessary adjustments to a plan. It also prevents the excessive expenditure of resources and unwanted changes in project or mission timelines. Although a project or task may completely change course, it is important to analyze how the current plan can be adapted to fit the circumstances.

Table 7-56. Identifies and adjusts to external influences

Strength Indicators	Need Indicators
Knows unit processes and the purpose of key policies, practices, and procedures.	Jumps to decisions based on the first answer that comes to mind.
Gathers and analyzes relevant information about the changing situation.	Collects information to form decisions until the window of opportunity closes.
Determines the causes, effects, and contributing factors to problems.	Is rigid and inflexible; refuses to be open to alternative ways of thinking.
Considers contingencies and their consequences.	Rejects the idea that external influences can derail a mission or tasking.
Maintains awareness of people and systems that could present obstacles to work accomplishment.	Refuses to give up a course of action when the mission or tasking changes.
Makes necessary, on-the-spot adjustments.	

Underlying Causes
Believes that there is only one viable solution; does not consider multiple solutions to a problem.
Believes that leaders must be decisive and tends to make decisions prematurely.
Is in search of the correct answers rather than the good enough solution; continues collecting data to inform decisionmaking well after the time for the required decision.
Does not operate well in high-stress situations.
Feels wedded to the original plan; is fearful of changing or modifying the plan midstream.

Table 7-56. Identifies and adjusts to external influences (continued)

Feedback	Brainstorm possible solutions to an external change as a group or team. Use the input to consider alternative ways of adjusting to external influences.
	Talk with superiors and peers about external factors that influence unit capabilities. Solicit feedback on factors that influence subordinates' ability to complete their work.
	Gain feedback from superiors, peers, or trusted subordinates on how well you demonstrate flexibility to alternative ways of thinking. Use the feedback to decide how you can become more open to new ideas.
	Request feedback from subordinates on how well you intervene and adjust their work. Do you provide appropriate and timely adjustments with clear direction?
Study	Identify new and emerging trends in an area of expertise, and research how the change will affect existing taskings and mission.
	Observe a unit that has undergone a major change due to an external factor, and document how they handled it. Use effective approaches or best practices.
	Reflect upon times when external influences negatively affected your performance or decisionmaking or team performance. What should you have done? Reflect upon times when you dealt more effectively with external influences. Why were you successful?
	Access the Virtual Improvement Center to complete: Removing Work Barriers, Being an Adaptable Leader in Times of Change, Out of Time: Managing Competing Demands.
Practice	If a mission or project is not on track, take a different action by devising creative solutions. Be open to the idea that there may be a better way.
	Talk with others inside and outside the chain of command to stay current on external influences that could affect the mission. Key opportunities to share information include attendance at conferences, conventions, and institutional training courses.
	Develop alternative strategies and solutions to accomplish an existing project or task. This serves as a contingency plan in case unexpected outcomes occur.
	Practice maintaining composure and managing frustration when external influences affect work. Remain focused on a positive outcome.
	Form or expand partnership with peers or others who get things done. Brainstorm ideas with them on identifying ways to adjust to outside influences that are currently affecting tasks and projects, as well as those that may affect tasks and projects in the future.

Glossary

AAR	after action review
ACT	Army Career Tracker
ACTEDS	Army Civilian Training Education and Development System
ADP	Army doctrinal publication
ADRP	Army doctrinal reference publication
ALDS	Army Leader Development Strategy
AR	Army regulation
ATP	Army techniques publication
CPT	captain
DA	Department of the Army
DA PAM	Department of the Army pamphlet
DOD	Department of Defense
FM	field manual
IDP	individual development plan
JP	joint publication
MSAF	Multi-Source Assessment and Feedback
NCO	noncommissioned officer
SOAR	situation, observation, associate and assess, and reinforce and recommend
U.S.	United States

SECTION II – TERMS

Army leader

Anyone who by virtue of assumed role or assigned responsibility inspires and influences people to accomplish organizational goals. Army leaders motivate people both inside and outside the chain of command to pursue actions, focus thinking and shape decisions for the greater good of the organization.(ADP 6-22)

*Army team building

A continuous process of enabling a group of people to reach their goals and improve their effectiveness through leadership and various exercises, activities and techniques.

leader development

The deliberate, continuous, sequential, and progressive process—founded in Army values—that grows Soldiers and Army Civilians into competent and confident leaders capable of decisive action. Leader development is achieved through the life-long synthesis of the knowledge, skills, and experiences gained through the training and educational opportunities in the institutional, operational, and self-development domains. (AR 350-1)

leadership

The process of influencing people by providing purpose, direction, and motivation to accomplish the mission and improve the organization. (ADP 6-22)

mentorship

The voluntary developmental relationship that exists between a person of greater experience and a person of lesser experience that is characterized by mutual trust and respect. (AR 600-100)

mission command

The exercise of authority and direction by the commander using mission orders to enable disciplined initiative within the commander's intent to empower agile and adaptive leaders in the conduct of unified land operations. (ADP 6-0)

References

REQUIRED PUBLICATIONS

These documents must be available to intended users of this publication.

Unless otherwise indicated, these are available on the Army Publishing Directorate (APD) web site (www.apd.army.mil).

Most joint publications are available online: http://www.dtic.mil/doctrine/new_pubs/jointpub.htm.

ADRP 1-02. *Terms and Military Symbols*. 2 February 2015.

JP 1-02. *Defense Dictionary of Military and Associated Terms*. 08 November 2010.

RELATED PUBLICATIONS

These sources contain relevant supplemental information.

Unless otherwise indicated, these are available on the Army Publishing Directorate (APD) web site (www.apd.army.mil).

ADP 5-0. *The Operations Process*. 17 May 2012.

ADP 6-0. *Mission Command*. 17 May 2012.

ADP 6-22. *Army Leadership*. 1 August 2012.

ADRP 1. *The Army Profession*. 14 June 2013.

ADRP 6-0. *Mission Command*. 17 May 2012.

ADRP 6-22. *Army Leadership*. 1 August 2012.

ADRP 7-0. *Training Units and Developing Leaders*. 23 August 2012.

AR 1-201. *Army Inspection Policy*. 25 February 2015.

AR 350-1. *Army Training and Leader Development*. 19 August 2014.

AR 600-20. *Army Command Policy*. 6 November 2014.

AR 600-100. *Army Leadership*. 8 March 2007.

AR 621-7. *Army Fellowships & Scholarships*. 8 August 1997.

AR 623-3. *Evaluation Reporting System*. 31 March 2014.

AR 690-950. *Career Management*. 31 Dec 2001.

Army Leader Development Strategy (ALDS). June 2013. Available at http://usacac.army.mil/cac2/CAL/repository/ALDS5June%202013Record.pdf.

ATP 2-33.4. *Intelligence Analysis*. 18 August 2014.

ATP 6-22.1. *The Counseling Process*. 1 July 2014.

DA PAM 600-3. *Commissioned Officer Professional Development and Career Management*. 3 December 2014.

DA PAM 600-25. *U.S. Army Noncommissioned Officer Professional Development Guide*. 28 July 2008.

DOD Instruction 1430.16. *Growing Civilian Leaders*. 19 November 2009. Available at http://dtic.mil/whs/directives/corres/ins1.html.

FM 27-10. *The Law of Land Warfare*. 18 July 1956.

PRESCRIBED FORMS

Unless otherwise indicated, DA Forms are available on the Army Publishing Directorate (APD) web site (www.apd.army.mil).

None.

REFERENCED FORMS

Unless otherwise indicated, DA Forms are available on the Army Publishing Directorate (APD) web site (www.apd.army.mil).

DA Form 2028. *Recommended Changes to Publications and Blank Forms.*

RECOMMENDED READINGS

These sources contain relevant supplemental information.
All URLs were accessed on 29 April 2015.
Some sites may require CAC authentication.

U.S. Center of Military History Professional Reading Lists. Available at www.history.army.mil/reading.html.

RECOMMENDED WEB SITES

All URLs were accessed on 29 April 2015.
Some sites may require CAC authentication.

All Army Activities (ALARACT) Messages. Available at https://www.us.army.mil/suite/page/550282.

Army 360 Multi-Source Assessment and Feedback (MSAF) Program. Available at https://msaf.army.mil/Home/LeadOn.aspx.

Army Career & Alumni Program (ACAP). Available at https://www.acap.army.mil.

Army Career Tracker (ACT). Available at https://actnow.army.mil.

Army Center for Enhanced Performance (ACEP). Available at: http://www.acep.army.mil/resources.html.

Army Civilian Training, Education & Development System (ACTEDS). Available at http://cpol.army.mil/library/train/acteds/.

Army Civilian Training & Leadership Development. Available at http://www.civiliantraining.army.mil/Pages/Homepage.aspx.

Army Credentialing Opportunities On-Line (COOL). Available at https://www.cool.army.mil.

ArmyFit. Available at https://armyfit.army.mil/.

Army Learning Management System (ALMS). Available at https://www.lms.army.mil.

Army Personnel Testing. Available at https://www.hrc.army.mil/site/education/APT.html.

Army Professional Forums. Available at https://www.milsuite.mil/book/community/spaces/apf.

Army Ready and Resilient. Available at: http://www.army.mil/readyandresilient.

Army Suicide Prevention Program. Available at http://www.armyg1.army.mil/hr/suicide.

Army Training and Certification Tracking System (ATCTS). Available at https://atc.us.army.mil.

Army Training Network (ATN). Available at https://atn.army.mil.

ATRRS Self-Development Center. Available at https://www.atrrs.army.mil/selfdevctr/eLearningWelcome.aspx.

Center for Army Leadership (CAL). Available at https://usacac.army.mil/cac2/CAL.

Center for Army Lessons Learned (CALL). Available at http://usacac.army.mil/cac2/call/index.asp.

Center for Army Profession and Ethic (CAPE). Available at http://cape.army.mil.

Central Army Registry (CAR). Available at https://atiam.train.army.mil/catalog/catalog/search.html.

Comprehensive Soldier & Family Fitness Program. Available at http://csf2.army.mil.

Congressional Medal of Honor Society. Available at http://www.cmohs.org/recipient-archive.php.

Digital Army Library Service (DALS). Available at http://www.libraries.army.mil.

FORSCOM Leader Development Toolbox. Available at http://www.forscom.army.mil/leaderdevelopment.

GoArmyEd. Available at https://www.goarmyed.com.

Human Resources Command (HRC). Available at www.hrc.army.mil.

Institute for NCO Professional Development (INCOPD). Available at http://www.tradoc.army.mil/INCOPD/index.html.

MILCONNECT Online Portal. Available at https://www.dmdc.osd.mil/milconnect.

Military OneSource. Available at http://www.militaryonesource.mil.

Military Personnel (MILPER) Messages. Available at https://www.hrc.army.mil/Milper.

Professional Development Toolkit. Available at http://www.army.mil/professional/.

Soldier for Life. Available at http://soldierforlife.army.mil.

U. S. Army Combat Readiness/Safety Center. Available at https://safety.army.mil/Default.aspx.

Virtual Improvement Center (VIC). Available at https://msaf.army.mil/My360/VIC/Default.aspx.

This page intentionally left blank.

Index

Entries are by paragraph unless specified otherwise.

Entries are by paragraph number unless stated otherwise.

Entries are by paragraph number unless stated otherwise.

This page intentionally left blank.

By Order of the Secretary of the Army

RAYMOND T. ODIERNO
General, United States Army
Chief of Staff

Official:

GERALD B. O'KEEFE
Administrative Assistant to the
Secretary of the Army
1513406

DISTRIBUTION:
Active Army, Army National Guard, and U.S. Army Reserve: To be distributed in accordance
with the initial distribution number (IDN) 110180, requirements for FM 6-22.

About Red Bike Publishing

Our company is registered as a government contractor company with the CCR and VetBiz (DUNS 826859691). Specifically we are a service disabled veteran owned small business. Red Bike Publishing provides high quality security books and republication of related Government regulations. Our books include the following which can be found at www.redbikepublishing.com and Amazon:

Army Topics

1. Ranger Handbook SH 21-76
2. US Army Physical Readiness Training TC 3.22-20
3. US Army Physical Fitness Training FM 21-20
4. US Army Leadership FM 6-22
5. US Army Drill and Ceremonies FM 3-21.5

National Security Topics

1. How to Win U.S. Government Contracts
2. Insider's Guide to Security Clearances
3. International Traffic in Arms Regulation (ITAR)
4. ISP Certification-The Industrial Security Professional Exam Manual
5. National Industrial Security Program Operating Manual (NISPOM)

Publishing

Get Rich in a Niche-The Insider's Guide to Self-Publishing in a Specialized Industry

www.ingramcontent.com/pod-product-compliance
Lightning Source LLC
Chambersburg PA
CBHW081417090426

42738CB00017B/3396